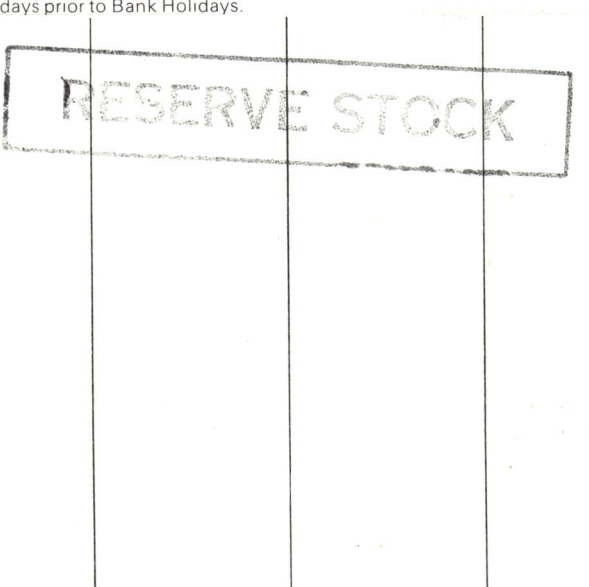

FAMOUS FRIGATE ACTIONS

"A THIRD TIME THE INTREPID OFFICER RETURNED TO THE ASSAULT."

FAMOUS FRIGATE ACTIONS

BY

CHARLES RATHBONE LOW

I.N., F.R.G.S.

AUTHOR OF "HER MAJESTY'S NAVY," "HISTORY OF THE INDIAN NAVY," "ENGLAND'S
SEA VICTORIES," "TALES OF OLD OCEAN," ETC., ETC.

WITH EIGHT ILLUSTRATIONS BY HERBERT K. ROOKE

CONWAY MARITIME PRESS
1970
LONDON

First printing   1898
Second printing 1970
Conway Maritime Press

SBN 85177 008 8

Printed in Great Britain by
Stephen Austin & Sons, Ltd., Hertford.

PREFACE.

THIS book has been written to supply an *hiatus* in our naval histories, and in compliance with a suggestion made in a criticism of a little companion volume, entitled "England's Sea Victories," written by me a few years ago. The latter work, as its name implies, dealt with the battles of the British Navy, and made no reference to the duels between single ships and the boat actions, which form almost as important a part of the naval history of our country as the fleet and squadron engagements, and, as regards the valour displayed by our officers and men, are perhaps even more remarkable. Some of these episodes, indeed, are as striking as anything told in the authentic history of warlike operations on sea or land. What can be more brilliant than the cutting out of the *Hermione*, of the *Chevrette*, of the *Cerbère*, and of the *Désirée*? What more glorious than the capture of the *Gamo*, of the *Hercule*, of the *Foudroyant*, of the *Pique*, of the *Forte*, and of the *Chesapeake*? These were victories, but sometimes even in defeat equal glory was won, as witness the capture of the *Leander* by the *Généreux*, of the *Nereid* by a French squadron, and numerous other instances. Every Briton knows of the death of the chivalrous Sir Richard Grenville, though it was not till the late Poet Laureate wrote his ode that this came about; but why should the equally glorious end of

other heroes be forgotten? Simply, I suppose, because,
as the classic poet says, the warriors who died before
Agamemnon had no bard like Homer to chronicle their
achievements.   Be it mine, though not in verse (this
I have striven to do in "Britannia's Bulwarks"), to
describe the deeds and the death of heroes like Hood,
Cooke, Faulknor, Bowen, Hardinge, Coombe, and
others as gallant, whose names have been relegated to
oblivion, because they were not admirals in command
of fleets at the time they sacrificed their lives for
their country, or died amid the glamour of a great
victory. An instance of a lack of appreciation has been
recently afforded by the action of the Dean and
Chapter of St. Paul's, who proposed to remove the
monument erected in 1802 by the King and Parliament to Captain Burges, of the *Ardent*, 74, who,
at the memorable victory achieved by Admiral
Duncan over the Dutch fleet at Camperdown, five
years before, broke the enemy's line and died in the
performance of the duty. It was actually proposed
that this hero's monument should be removed from
the south aisle and banished to the crypt, to make
room for the monument privately subscribed by
friends to the memory of Lord Leighton. The *Times*
adequately described the proposal as "grotesque," and
it was defeated by an indignant public opinion.   But
what shall we say for the patriotism of the Englishmen
who could have made it ?   This book is a slight and
inadequate literary monument to the naval worthies
I have named in its pages.

C. R. Low.

82, Elsham Road, Kensington

CONTENTS.

———

CHAPTER I.

CHAPTER III.

CHAPTER IV.

CHAPTER V.

CHAPTER VI.

CHAPTER VII.

LIST OF ILLUSTRATIONS.

FAMOUS FRIGATE ACTIONS.

CHAPTER I.

IN the history of the British Navy the most important portion is that which deals with the battles between our fleets and those of rival Powers; but not less interesting to the reader are the duels between single ships, and as the line-of-battle ships sailed in squadrons or fleets, it happened that the smaller vessels—the corvettes, sloops-of-war, and

B

brigs, but more especially the frigates, which roamed the sea singly, either to protect our commerce or harry that of the enemy—were frequently engaged with vessels of like force. These combats, which were generally of a sanguinary and hard-fought character, afforded even more scope for the individual skill of the commanders, if not for the daring of the officers and men, than the great contests between the fleets composed of stately ships-of-the-line. It is the most important among these numberless duels which it is my object to describe in these pages.

I will pass over with a mere mention the desperate action, in 1512, between the *Regent*, flying the flag of Sir Thomas Knivet, second-in-command of the fleet under Sir Edward Howard, which engaged the French near Brest, on which occasion our admiral grappled with the *Cordelier*, of the same force, also a flagship, when both the ships caught fire and blew up, the crews still fighting desperately. On this occasion the British loss was 700 and that of the French 900, with both the admirals. Very sanguinary, also, was the action between the flagship of Sir Edward Howard, Lord High Admiral of the Navy, and that of the French commander-in-chief, which took place soon after, when Howard led his men in person on to the deck of the enemy as the two ships lay alongside of each other. Unfortunately the ships parted, and the French seamen, rallying from their panic, overpowered and slew the English admiral and his handful of seamen. Lord Cochrane (or Lord Dundonald, as he afterwards became) was a great admirer of this daring officer, and used to repeat with approval a dogma of his that "a sailor to be good for anything must be mad," and if insanity is synonymous with utter recklessness, the brilliant seaman who captured by boarding the Spanish frigate with the crew of the little brig *Speedy* was "as mad as a March hare," or as Lord High Admiral Howard.

There were no frigate actions in the war with Spain, which began with the despatch of the great Armada to subjugate these islands, though every one will recall the memorable fight between Sir Richard Grenville and 53 Spanish ships off the Azores, when after a resistance probably unsurpassed for obstinacy in the annals of naval war, the *Revenge* was compelled to strike, but not until she was reduced to a mere wreck, with her decks and quarters cumbered with the dead and dying. The unequal fight was maintained from three in the afternoon till midnight, by which time the British crew had sunk the *St. Philip*, of 78 guns, and though boarded by four Spaniards, drove them off, sinking one of the ships. Sir Richard, who had been wounded, would not leave the deck to have his injury dressed, when he was again wounded in the head, the surgeon being killed at his side. The admiral was carried on board the

Spanish flagship, where he expired two days afterwards, and the *Revenge*, which he had commanded
so nobly, sank at sea, carrying with her the prize
crew of 200 men, so that altogether the "Dons"
paid somewhat dearly for their riddled and blood-
stained prize. This incident, so well known to writers
on British naval history, had been consigned to
oblivion by the general reader till its memory was
revived by Tennyson's noble ode, and it is never
likely to be again forgotten.

Before leaving the question of the war with Spain
it is perhaps right to say that there has been a good
deal of exaggeration among contemporary writers as
to the comparative strength of the ships and arma-
ments of the English and Spanish fleets. This
impairs but little the estimate we must form of the
heroism of Drake and his fellows, who thought
little of odds, and were of the opinion of Nelson,
who said that "you can never do wrong if you lay
your ship alongside the nearest Frenchman." Professor Laughton, who has done so much to elucidate
our early naval history from original records, on this
point of the relative size of ships and weight of
metal of the fleets engaged in Philip II.'s unsuccessful attempt to invade England in 1588, shows
that between the largest Spanish and the largest
English ships there was no appreciable difference in
tonnage, though the Spanish ships, from their lofty

poops and forecastles, looked bigger. These huge erections, which gave them an advantage in hand-to-hand fighting, were otherwise much against them, as for these unwieldy craft to work to windward was almost impossible. The strength of their crews has also been much overstated, but the most extraordinary exaggeration has been in the weight of their ordnance. It now appears, both from Spanish records and from our own State papers, that the armament of the Spanish ships was not only not greater than ours, but was, indeed, smaller; that, to take one instance, the *Capitana* of Pedro de Valdes, of 1,150 tons, one of the largest and most powerful ships in the fleet, threw a broadside of about 195 pounds. After she was captured she was sent into Torbay, where an exact inventory of her guns and stores was taken, and we have thus positive knowledge of her armament. On the other hand, the English *Triumph,* of the same size, threw a broadside of more than 400 pounds, and even the English ships of 500 tons carried a broadside weight of metal of more than 250 pounds. Going lower in the scale, many of the Spanish ships of 600 or 700 tons had little effective armament, and, according to Professor Laughton, were certainly inferior to our ships of 200 tons as long as they were kept at a distance. The Spanish tactics were to close and board; but that, from their inferiority of sailing, especially "on a wind," they failed to do. Counting the opposing force on these lines, the Spaniards brought into the Channel about 62 effective ships, exclusive of the four *galeases*. Three vessels and one of the *galeases* they had lost before the 29th of July, the day of the great fight off Gravelines, so that in the decisive battle the Spaniards mustered 59 ships and three *galeases*, against 49 English ships of over 200 tons. They fell into disorder, got entangled, and were terribly mauled, several being sunk outright, and several others being driven ashore on the coast of Flanders, which was due, not to fortuitous circumstances, but to the daring and superior skill of our seamen, led by heroic souls like Drake, Howard, Frobisher, and Hawkins. The main body of their fleet fled to the North, and suffered terrible losses in bad weather on the coast of Ireland, a bare half of their original number getting back to Spain. All this points to one conclusion, that preparation and practical experience of the sea is certain to give the victory where other conditions are at all equal, and hence it is a wise policy, though it may be a more expensive one, that keeps our ships constantly at sea, while those of the Continental Powers are mostly laid up in port. When the time of trial comes, the officers and seamen who have been trained at sea, instead of theoretically in naval barracks, will, as in the past, carry all before them.

During the wars with the Dutch in Cromwell's

time and in the reign of Charles II. we have only
mention of one frigate action, though, perhaps, no
maritime war waged before or since is so replete with
sanguinary and hard-fought battles between fleets.
As grand, if not as memorable, as the death of Sir
Richard Grenville was that of Sir William Berkeley
and Lord Sandwich, and also of Admirals Spragge
and Myngs, some of whom rest within Westminster
Abbey, where the monuments over their remains
record their services to our country. Sir William
Berkeley, who was killed at the age of 27, was vice-
admiral of the fleet in the four days' engagement
with the Dutch fleet in June, 1666. His ship, the
Swiftsure—always a famous name in our naval history, one of the same name being captured by the
French 150 years later under somewhat similar circumstances—was cut off from the main body in the
first day's action, and was compelled to surrender to
the Dutch fleet. This was the manner of the British
admiral's death, as told in the "Life of Van
Tromp": "Highly to be admired was the resolution
of Vice-Admiral Berkeley, who, though cut off from
the line, surrounded by his enemies, great numbers
of his men killed, his ship disabled and boarded on
all sides, yet continued fighting almost alone, killed
several with his own hand, and would accept of no
quarter till, at length, being shot in the throat with
a musket-ball, he retired into the captain's cabin,

where he was found dead, extended at full length
on a table, and almost covered with his own
blood."

Equally noble was the manner of the death of
Lord Sandwich, in the memorable battle off Solebay
on the 28th May, 1672 ; of Sir Christopher Myngs
in the engagement when Berkeley fell ; and of Sir
Edward Spragge in the last battle of the war with
Holland, on the 17th August, 1673, when he singled
out and engaged the flagship of Cornelius Van Tromp,
till his own was rendered unmanageable, when he
shifted his flag, Tromp having done so no less than
three times, and his boat was struck by a round-shot
and he was drowned as he was proceeding for the
second time to a fresh ship to renew the battle with
his brave adversary.

During the course of the war a frigate action was
fought between the *Tiger*, of 40 guns, Captain Harman, and the *Schaerlaes*, of 36 guns, Captain de
Witt, which was at the time refitting at Cadiz. The
Tiger, having arrived at the port, the British and
Dutch commanders agreed to fight in the open sea
for the honour of their respective flags, just as, in
1813, Captain Broke, of the *Shannon*, and Captain
Lawrence, of the Yankee frigate *Chesapeake*, came to
terms to fight off Boston harbour, and, it may be
added, with the same result. A day was fixed in
both instances, and in one the citizens of Cadiz, as

in the other those of Boston, witnessed the combat
which took place sufficiently near the land to afford
a distant view of the cannonade. The ships were
well matched, for though the *Tiger* carried four more
guns, the Dutch frigate had the superiority in pos-
sessing a stronger crew by 90 men, and the similarity
between the frigate actions I have named was still
further carried out in the length of the engagement,
for both of the enemy's frigates were carried by
boarding within a quarter of an hour of the time the
first shot was fired. As off Boston the seamen,
carefully trained by Captain Broke, were superior
gunners to those of the *Chesapeake*, so at Cadiz the
tars of the *Tiger* had brought their gunnery practice
to great perfection under the eye of Captain (afterwards Admiral Sir John) Harman, one of the best
officers of the race trained by Blake. In these typical
cases it was proved by the inexorable logic of facts
that good gunnery is the first of all requirements in
the training of the man-of-war's man ; and as in the
last war with France it was the training in great
gun drill by Sir John Jervis, afterwards Lord St.
Vincent, that made the British seaman irresistible—
as Nelson, who had served under Jervis, was the first
to own—so it was neglect of the art of gunnery
subsequently to Trafalgar, the last of the great battles
between fleets (though there were minor encounters
later, as that at St. Domingo), which even more

than a relaxation in discipline and overweening belief
in the navy's invincibility, consequent on our unbroken
series of victories, which conduced to the unfortunate
series of defeats that befell our frigates in their encounters with those of the United States, though we
may add in palliation of these disasters that in almost
every instance our ships and crews fought under the
disadvantage of inferiority in armament and numerical
strength.

The action between the *Tiger* and *Schaerlaes* was a
very one-sided affair.   In his first broadside Captain
Harman shot away the Dutchman's mainmast, when,
laying his ship alongside the enemy in the good old
fashion, for it had the merit of antiquity even in the
days of the " Merrie Monarch," the gallant captain led
his men on board the *Schaerlaes*, and, driving the
enemy below after a brief resistance, hauled down the
flag of the United Provinces, and hoisted in its stead
the Cross of St. George.

From the day, early in 1674, when peace was concluded between this country and Holland, not a shot
was fired in anger between the nations till 1797,
when Admiral Duncan defeated and destroyed the
Dutch fleet at the memorable battle of Camperdown,
which gained him a peerage, as in the same year
Jervis's victory over the Spanish fleet off Cape St.
Vincent gave him the title by which he is best known
in history.   With William III. as King of England,

a definite peace and alliance was concluded with
Holland, and our navy, which had been on amicable
terms with that of France during the Stuart era, again
returned to that condition of hostility with the Gallic
fleet, which may be almost regarded as our normal
state since the days of Cressy and Sluys.

On the 15th of May, 1689, took place the indecisive
action off Bantry Bay, for which Admiral Herbert, for
political rather than professional reasons, was created
Earl of Torrington, and on the 30th of June, in the
following year, was fought another important engagement off Beachy Head, which, owing chiefly to our
numerical inferiority, ended in something like a defeat,
though the French commander, De Tourville, was not
possessed of sufficient enterprise to follow up his
success, and Lord Torrington was enabled by his
masterly arrangements to defend the Thames, and
prevent his opponent from reaping the fruits of his
victory, if such it may be called.   Lord Torrington
was tried for his conduct, and though acquitted of
blame was not again employed afloat, and Admiral
Russell succeeded to the command.   Before leaving
this officer—who after being over-rewarded for Bantry
Head was unduly depreciated for his failure at
Beachy Head, for which indeed he was little to blame,
and where, according to some competent critics,
Admiral P. Colomb among the number, he displayed
some of the qualities of a great commander—we should

mention briefly an action he fought with a Dutch frigate. Captain Herbert, while in command of the *Pembroke* frigate, in March, 1667, during the war with Holland, engaged a ship of equal force, and the following is a quaint contemporary account of the action. "Captain Herbert, in the *Pembroke*, is now in this port, being newly returned from a fresh dispute with a Zealand man-of-war, of 34 guns and 180 men, with whom he fought some days before from two in the afternoon till night put an end to that day's work. All that night the *Pembroke* frigate, carrying out a light for the Zealander, and the next morning, being to the windward, fired a gun and bore up to re-engage her; but the Zealander, being the nimbler sailer, bore away once or twice before the wind, declining any further dispute, which the frigate perceiving, and fearing to be put to leeward of the port by a fruitless pursuit, the wind then blowing a strong levant, came again from the bay, which the Zealander wanted not the confidence to boast of as a mark of his victory. Since this, the frigate being put ashore to wash and tallow, the Zealander made several challenges, but went out to sea again before the frigate could get ready. Yesterday morning the Zealander coming in, the frigate being ready went out to meet him, and passed five times upon him within pistol shot, and the Zealander finding the service too hot bore in for the bay, pursued for a long time by the frigate, being unable to overtake him, fired her chase gun, and stood out again to sea."

Admiral Russell, two years after Beachy Head, gained a great victory over De Tourville off Cape la Hogue, his flag officers being Sir Cloudesley Shovel and Sir George Rooke, two among the most famous names in our naval history; and Rooke, a few days after the battle, with his boats destroyed 13 of the enemy's ships. A frigate squadron, commanded by Commodore Killigrew, of the *Plymouth*, of 60 guns, fought an action on the 18th January, 1695, with a French squadron, and though Killigrew was killed, his frigates captured two 60-gun ships, the *Content* and *Trident*. Still more memorable was the action in which the famous Admiral Benbow was mortally wounded. On the 19th August, 1702, Benbow, with his flag in the *Breda*, of 70 guns, and having six frigates under his command, sighted a French squadron of four large ships and six smaller ones off Carthagena, in the West Indies, under Admiral du Casse, and engaged the enemy. Though he received little assistance from his captains, Benbow kept close to the enemy, and, on the following morning at daybreak, found himself unsupported save by the *Ruby*, 48 guns, Captain Walton, the rest of his squadron being some miles astern. On the 21st August the *Breda* and *Ruby* engaged the enemy, the five other frigates taking no part in the action, though repeatedly signalled by the admiral to do so. The unequal fight was continued for three days, the *Breda* being partially assisted by the *Falmouth*, the *Ruby*, which was disabled, having been despatched to Port Royal. For a long time the *Breda* bore the French fire, until, at length, being in too crippled a state to continue the chase, she bore up for Jamaica and Du Casse returned to Carthagena. A court-martial was convened to try the cowardly captains, two of whom were sentenced to death and shot on board the *Bristol*, and a third only escaped a like fate by dying before the trial. Benbow had been wounded severely in the face and arm while boarding Du Casse's flagship, and afterwards had his leg shot off, and succumbed to his wounds. He left a reputation in the navy as an officer of undaunted courage, one every inch a seaman, and a strict disciplinarian; in fact, a regular sea-dog of the school of Drake and Grenville, of which so many examples may be cited in the great war with France.

Among famous frigate captains who took many French prizes were Lord Dursley, afterwards Earl of Berkeley and head of the Admiralty, and Captain Tollet of the *Assurance*, 70 guns, who, with two other 50-gun ships, engaged four French sail off the Lizard Point. Tollet and the French Commodore Duguai-Trouin engaged yard-arm to yard-arm, and a desperate battle took place, until the *Assurance* being almost a wreck, the French squadron escaped. Lord Dursley, on his part, engaged the same redoubtable adversary, who was then flying his flag in the *Achille*—a name which is seen in the list of both the French and British fleets at Trafalgar, one having being previously captured by us—which was greatly shattered and only escaped capture by her swiftness; while Lord Dursley recovered the *Bristol*, which had been taken the day before, and captured the *Gloire*, of 44 guns and 312 men, his own loss in the action having been 70 killed and wounded. In the same year (1709) the *Falmouth*, 50, Captain Ryddel, while convoying some English merchantmen, was attacked near Scilly by a French squadron of four ships, and a desperate action ensued between the *Falmouth* and the French commander's ship of 60 guns, which was beaten off by the gallant Ryddel, who brought the convoy safe into Plymouth, with the loss of his second lieutenant and 13 men killed, and 56, including himself, wounded.

Two years later Captain Walpole, in the *Lion*, recaptured, after a severe action, in which he lost 40 men, the *Pembroke*, 50, formerly of the British navy. It is only necessary to mention the capture of the French 50-gun frigate *Toulouse*, by the *Hampton Court* of like force, after a spirited action, as Captain Mighells was assisted by another frigate. One of the most famous and successful frigate captains was Sir William Jumper, who, with Captains Hicks and Whitaker, was chiefly instrumental in the capture of

Gibraltar, in 1704, when they landed from the fleet with a strong party of seamen and held the Mole till reinforced against all the persistent attacks of the Spaniards, though 100 British men were blown up by the explosion of a mine. His services in 1694-96, while in command of the *Weymouth*, frigate, were most meritorious. He captured the *Invincible* after a running fight, and many privateers, which had been preying on British commerce, and also the *Fougueux*, 48, and engaged another 50-gun frigate, which would also have been taken but that the *Weymouth* caught fire, when the enemy escaped.

In 1713 was concluded the Peace of Utrecht with France, and, save Sir George Byng's famous victory over the Spanish fleet off Messina, the navy saw little service for some years, though we should chronicle a brilliant capture made by the *Hind*, 20, Captain Dalgarno, of a Sallie rover of 24 guns, when the enemy was so damaged by the *Hind's* fire that she sank a few hours after striking her flag. Of the same character was a success achieved by Captain (after-wards Admiral Sir Challoner) Ogle, commanding the *Swallow*, off Cape Lopez on the West African coast. Captain Ogle disguised his ship to represent a merchantman, and on sighting three piratical craft, under the command of a noted buccaneer, one Roberts, pretended to fly and was chased to sea by one of the freebooters, on which he turned when far from land,

and, after a spirited action, captured her. Now returning with the black flag hoisted over the English ensign, he was met by the other two pirate vessels, who came out to greet their victorious comrade, but Captain Ogle, throwing off the mask, ran up the ensign to the peak and opening fire compelled both to strike, though not until Roberts was killed. The survivors of the piratical crews, numbering 160, were brought to trial at Cape Coast Castle, and of those condemned to death 52 were executed, and their bodies were left hanging in chains at several points on the coast—a ghastly and salutary warning to evildoers and others inclined to embark on similar courses.

Among the most famous officers of the British Navy was Lord Anson. In 1740 Commodore Anson sailed from Plymouth with five ships-of-war to attack the Philippines and other Spanish possessions in the Pacific Ocean, and, after encountering incredible dangers and hardships, which are all told in admirable style in the history of his voyage round the world, the expedition was reduced to his ship alone, the *Centurion*, of 50 guns, having then only 201 men on board, more than half having perished since he sailed from England with the squadron under his command. The *Centurion* had been cruising about three weeks off the Philippine Islands, when, on the 20th June, 1743, was sighted the Spanish galleon, *Senhora del Caba Donga*, returning from Acapulco, stored with

C

bullion and silver coin. The officers and crew were
overjoyed at the prospect of having at length some
recompense for all the trials and sufferings they had
endured during the past three years ; and though the
Spanish crew numbered 550 men, they entered upon
the conflict without a doubt as to the result, so confident were they in their own valour and the skill of
their commander, while for the Spanish Admiral Montero and his crew, their feelings may be imagined as,
after crossing the ocean, they found the British frigate,
like a lion across their path, ready to dispute their
entry into the port where they were to land the price-
less cargo. However, there was nothing to do for the
honour of their flag and the safety of their cargo but
to fight, and they doubtless were confident of their
ability to dispose of their antagonist, as, besides a crew
of thrice her strength, the galleon carried 42 heavy
and 28 lighter pieces of ordnance. Manœuvring his
ship with skill, Commodore Anson fired a broadside
when the Spaniard was within pistol-shot range, and
so accurate and destructive was his fire that in two
hours' time Admiral Montero struck his flag, having
lost 67 killed and 84 wounded, the loss of the *Centurion* being only 19. Besides a cargo of cochineal
valued at £313,000, the galleon carried over 1,300,000
" pieces of eight," and 35,000 ounces of silver bullion,
all of which became the prize of the victors. Commodore Anson sailed for Canton and Macao, and

having provisioned his ship and sold the galleon, he continued on his voyage of circumnavigation, and on the 15th June, 1744, the *Centurion* cast anchor at Spithead, nearly four years after sailing from that port, two others of the five vessels forming his squadron having returned after proceeding no farther than the South American coast.

In March, 1744, war was declared against France, and in the following June the British navy sustained a loss in the capture of the *Northumberland,* Captain Watson, carrying 70 guns and 480 men, which was captured after sustaining the fire for three hours of two French ships-of-the-line and a frigate. Captain Watson was mortally wounded in the action, and the unfortunate officer to whose lot it fell to surrender the ship was tried by court-martial and sentenced to imprisonment for life in the Marshalsea Prison.

In the following year, 1745, took place a desperate battle between the *Lion,* 58, Captain Brett, and the *Elizabeth,* 64, which was convoying the *Doutelle,* a small frigate conveying Prince Charles Edward on his ill-starred expedition to Scotland, which ended in the disaster of Culloden, and was the last attempt made by the Stuarts to recover the throne of their ancestors. Soon after losing sight of the French coast the *Lion* —one of those ubiquitous British frigates whose sleepless vigilance Napoleon so bitterly complained of in Egypt, after Nelson's victory at the Nile, and at

Bordeaux when a fugitive from Waterloo—hove in sight and brought the *Elizabeth* to action. Captain Brett was not aware of the presence of the Pretender on board the smaller vessel—which, crowding sail, escaped and reached Scotland in safety—and engaged the *Elizabeth*. A desperate duel ensued for five hours at close quarters, but the frigates were so equally matched that at the end of that period, exhausted with their fruitless efforts to achieve victory, and reduced almost to the condition of a wreck, they parted company. Both had lost heavily, the *Lion* having 150 men killed and wounded, and the *Elizabeth* over 200, and she was, moreover, compelled to returned to Belleisle to refit and repair the damages to her shattered hull.

The following is the official account of this memorable action :—"His Majesty's ship the *Lion*, of 58 guns, being in the latitude of 47° 57″ north, and west from the meridian of the Lizard 39 leagues, Captain Brett, her commander, saw two sail to leeward, to which he immediately bore down, and by three in the afternoon found them to be two of the enemy's ships. By four o'clock he was within two miles of them, when they hoisted French colours and shortened sail. One of them was a man-of-war of 64 guns, and the other a ship of 16 guns. At five the *Lion* ran alongside the large ship, and began to engage within pistol-shot. The ships continued in

that situation till ten, during which time they kept a
continual fire at each other, when the *Lion's* rigging
being cut to pieces, her mizen-mast, main-top-mast,
main-yard, fore-topsail-yard, and main-topsail-yard
shot away, all her lower masts and top-masts shot
through in many places, so that she lay muzzled on
the sea, and could do nothing with her sails, the
French ship sheered off and in less than an hour was
out of sight, the *Lion* not being able to follow her.
The small ship in the beginning of the engagement
made two attempts to rake the *Lion*, but was soon
beat off by her stern chase, and after that lay off at a
great distance. Forty-five of the *Lion's* men were killed
outright, and 107 wounded, seven of whom died of
their wounds soon after. Captain Brett was wounded
and much bruised in the arm ; his master lost his right
arm, and his lieutenants were all wounded ; nevertheless, they would not leave the deck, excepting the
first lieutenant, who was so much hurt that he was
obliged to be carried off." In a private letter from
the Hague the writer says of the action : "The fight
lasted nine hours, but night coming on the *Elizabeth*,
quite disabled, got away to Brest ; the captain and
64 men were killed, 136 dangerously wounded, and a
great number slightly. She had on board £400,000
sterling and arms for several thousand men." Thus
if Captain Brett was unsuccessful in capturing the
Pretender, he cut off a large part of the sinews of

war with which he intended to arm his adherents in
Ireland and Scotland. The English Government had
no more trouble with the Pretender, whose claims on
the Crown had kept the country in a flutter of anxiety
for many years past.

In the preceding year a fleet of 29 sail was
gathered in the Downs under the command of the
veteran Admiral Sir John Norris, as the French had
assembled 23 sail at Brest with the object of invading
Scotland in the interests of the Stuart prince. Speak-
ing of Sir John Norris, one of the most famous
admirals of a time that boasted Hawke, Anson,
Hughes, and Boscawen, it should be noted that while
in command of the *Orford* he captured, after a smart
action, the French frigate *Hazard*, of 52 guns and
400 men. A noted frigate action was that between
the *Tartar*, Captain Lockhart-Ross (one of the most
enterprising officers of his day), carrying 24 guns and
200 men, and the *Melampe*, of 36 guns and 300 men,
specially fitted out to capture the *Tartar*, whose
depredations on French commerce and daring in
engaging ships of superior force had made her the
dread of the enemy. The *Melampe* struck her flag
after an obstinate resistance, but with great treachery
her commander made a desperate attempt to carry the
Tartar by boarding, when he was repulsed with the
loss of 50 men, who were either killed or drowned in
the attempt.

Very glorious for British arms was the action between the 74's *Nottingham* and *Magnanime*, which struck after losing 150 men, and equally resultless and almost as sanguinary as the duel between the *Lion* and *Elizabeth* was an action off Rochefort between the *Colchester*, 50, Captain O'Brien, assisted by the corvette *Lyme*, 20, and the French frigates *Aquilon*, 48, and *Fidelle*, 36. It was not until about six o'clock in the evening of the 17th May, 1756, that the ships reached within cannon-shot range of each other, and soon after they came to close quarters. The *Colchester* and *Aquilon* engaged with the utmost fury till past midnight, but neither gained any advantage over the other, and gradually the fire slackened, till having done all that was demanded by the honour of their respective flags, they ceased firing to repair damages, and the combat was not renewed. The *Lyme* had a more unequal task with her superior opponent, but her officers and crew did their duty, and they also parted company with honour satisfied.

As in the case of the *Northumberland*, the *Warwick*, 60, Captain Shuldham, was compelled to strike to three French ships of equal force, after a severe and protracted action in which her gallant commander and a large number of her crew were slain. The *Warwick* was subsequently recaptured, and her loss was in a measure counterbalanced by the capture, by the *Norwich* and *Lichfield,* of the *Arc-en-Ciel,* 50 guns, carrying troops and warlike stores from Louisburg, in Cape Breton Island, off which in the previous year the *Dunkirk,* Captain Howe, the famous admiral who gained the battle in 1794 known as the "Glorious First of June," in company with the *Defence,* Captain Andrews, captured the *Alcide* and *Lys,* all the vessels engaged being of 60 guns.

The Treaty of Aix-la-Chapelle, in 1748, had merely patched up a peace between England and France, and within seven years the countries were again involved in a war which, for its events at sea and on the continents of Europe, Asia, and America, and the conquests made, was one of the most glorious ever waged by this country. Before the close of the "Seven Years' War," which convulsed Europe and made vast and enduring changes in its political divisions, England had established her supremacy in India and conquered Canada, besides making her naval ascendency unquestioned in Europe. Two naval captains, Forrest, of the *Augusta,* and Tyrrell, of the *Buckingham,* greatly distinguished themselves in the war; and while the former with three frigates engaged off Jamaica four French ships of the same class and beat them off after an obstinate engagement, Tyrrell engaged the *Florissant,* carrying 14 more guns than his ship, in a desperate fight, the sea running high at the time. Tyrrell was wounded in the action and resigned the command to his first lieutenant, Marshall, who was soon after slain, when the second lieutenant continued the battle with unflagging spirit at close quarters until the *Florissant* lowered her colours. Altogether this was one of the most memorable actions, whether as regarded obstinacy or loss of life, recorded in our naval history, for the *Florrisant* had no less than 180 killed and 300 wounded, and was so damaged in her hull that she could with difficulty be brought into port. As was the custom in our wars with the French, the British seamen directed their fire mostly on the hull to force the enemy to surrender, while "Johnny Crapeau," as Jack called his adversary, aimed chiefly at the rigging of his foe so as to cripple him with the object of making his escape. It was scarcely surprising that while one combatant thus acted mostly on the defensive, he was seldom successful in repelling the attack of his bolder and more self-reliant opponent.

But even more glorious, because the disparity was greater, was the action in the Mediterranean between the *Monmouth*, 64, Captain Arthur Gardiner, and the *Foudroyant*, 80, flying the flag of Admiral du Quesne. Captain Gardiner had a grudge against the ship, for while he was flag-captain of the unfortunate Admiral Byng on board the *Ramillies*, in the action off Minorca, which resulted in Byng's defeat and subsequent execution, the *Foudroyant* on that occasion carried the flag of de Galissoniere, the French admiral. Gardiner had often been heard to declare that if ever he encountered the *Foudroyant* he would tackle her no matter under what terms of inferiority as regards force, and now his wish was gratified, and he eagerly prepared to redeem his word ; yet the disparity was enough to deter most men from the venture, for he could scarcely hope for success when the *Foudroyant's* 42- and 22-pounders were pitted against his 12 and 24's, the respective broadside weight of metal being 1,036 pounds and 540, while as regards complement the Frenchman had 1,000 men on board and the gallant little *Monmouth* only 470. But nothing daunted, the gallant Gardiner trusted that his men would carry him triumphantly through the ordeal, and he was warranted by the event. The battle commenced about 8 P.M. on the 27th April, 1758, and was fought throughout the dark hours of night till nearly one o'clock, when Admiral du Quesne hauled down his flag, though, sad to say, the honour of accepting his sword did not fall to the lot of Captain Gardiner. Within an hour of the commencement of the action he was shot through the head by a musket-ball ; but before resigning the command he exacted a promise from his first lieutenant that he would never surrender the ship ; and nobly the officer kept his word, for, nailing the British flag to the staff, he swore that if any man

ACTION BETWEEN THE "MONMOUTH" AND THE "FOUDROYANT."

attempted to strike it he would shoot him.* At
first fortune seemed against our countrymen, for soon
after the captain was mortally wounded the *Mon-*
mouth's mizen-mast was shot away—an event hailed
by the enemy with cheers; but the British crew re-
taliated by shooting over the side the *Foudroyant's*
mizen-mast, and added to their score by sending
the main-mast to follow it. This infused fresh ardour
in our men, while the enemy suffered from corre-
sponding depression of spirits, which told on the
rapidity and accuracy of their fire; and at length,
driven from the guns, they struck the white flag of
France, and the *Foudroyant* became a British prize.

Ever since that glorious day a ship of that name
has been borne on the books of our navy, and one
was Nelson's favourite flag-ship, and with him on
board, and later under the command of Captain Berry,
assisted at the capture of two 74's, the *Généreux* and
Guillaume Tell, the only ships which had escaped
from the Nile.†

* Though Lieutenant Carkett displayed such gallantry on this
memorable occasion, it is no less strange than true that in Rodney's
indecisive action with De Guichen in the West Indies, on the 17th
April, 1780, he behaved badly and was brought to court-martial, and
only escaped dismissal because of his previous good conduct.

† This *Foudroyant,* the third of the name to fly the Union Jack,
was launched in 1798, and last year (1896) the writer enjoyed the
privilege of inspecting her as she lay off Gravesend, rigged and with
her guns on board, recalling in some degree her condition when, as
a smart 80-gun ship, she bore the flag of our greatest admiral. May
the name never die out in the navy!

This year, 1758, was a memorable one for single-ship victories, as on the 29th May, a month after the capture of the *Foudroyant*, the *Raisonnable*, carrying 64 guns and 630 men, surrendered to the *Dorsetshire*, 70, Captain Dennis, after a desperate action in which the enemy had 160 men placed *hors de combat;* and it is an interesting circumstance that the first ship in which Nelson served was the *Raisonnable*, 64, under the command of his uncle, Captain Suckling, the second of the name, that taken by Captain Dennis having been wrecked in the West Indies. In the following year the *Boreas*, frigate, another ship identified with Nelson, as he commanded her when a young post-captain, engaged in the West Indies the *Sirène*, commanded by Commodore McCartie, an Irish officer in the French service, and captured her after a spirited engagement ; and about the same time four other frigates of the same squadron to which the *Sirène* belonged were all captured or forced ashore by some ships of Admiral Holmes' fleet on the Jamaica station.

The great French writer, Voltaire, when reviewing the result of this and previous naval wars between his country and England, arrived at the sorrowful conclusion that the inferiority of the Frenchman to the Briton on the ocean was due to the fact that "the French can live well enough without the sea, which is essentially necessary to the English ; and the nations always succeed best in those things for which they have an absolute occasion." And he also asks if our incontestable superiority may not be attributable to our climate, which " produces men of a more steady resolution and of a more vigorous constitution than that of France." The late Charles Kingsley was apparently of the same opinion as regards the influence of our more vigorous climate on the English character, for he declared that the east wind was a potent factor in making John Bull the sturdy and resolute character he is.

Of actions between single ships during the war, passing over minor affairs with privateers and small craft, we will mention the capture by the *Vestal*, 32, Captain Hood, of the *Bellone*, her superior in men and guns, after a well-fought engagement of two hours ; and of the *Danaë*, 40, by two smaller frigates, the *Southampton* and *Melampe*, herself a prize as her name denotes. Off Cape Finisterre also the *Achilles*, 60, Captain Barrington, engaged the *Comte de St. Florentine*, of equal force, when for two hours the battle raged with unabated spirit till the French commander was slain, and 116 of his men were killed or wounded, when her flag was struck and she with difficulty was brought into Plymouth, so riddled was her hull with shot. About the same time Captain Faulknor, of the *Windsor*, 60, engaged four ships which, once having belonged to the French

East India Company, had been fitted with guns like
men-of-war, and forced the sternmost one, named the
Duc de Chartres, to strike her colours, but the others
managed to make good their escape.   The odds
were the other way when the French 32-gun frigate
Arethuse found herself in the presence of the *Venus*
and *Thames;* and after a very gallant defence, in
which she lost 60 of her crew, her captain, the Marquis
de Vaudreuil, was fain to surrender, having done all
that the most scrupulous code of honour could have
demanded of a French aristocrat of the old school.

Some idea of the success achieved by the British
navy during the war may be gathered by the statement that, during the year 1760 alone, our fleet
captured 27 ships-of-the-line and 27 frigates, which
were all added to the navy, destroying besides eight
battle-ships and four frigates ; while during the same
period our loss had been only seven sail-of-the-line
and five frigates.   On the other hand, as our trade
was of much greater volume than that of the French,
notwithstanding all the exertions of our cruisers, no
less than 210 trading vessels had been lost to 165
captured from the enemy.   At this time also, it may
be noted as some indication of the patriotic fervour
of our people, though the population of England and
Scotland could scarcely have exceeded nine millions,
120 sail-of-the-line, besides frigates, and 70,000
seamen and marines, were voted for the year's service.

During the year 1761 the *Richard*, Captain Elphinstone, carrying 32 guns and 220 men, engaged off the Hague the French frigate *Felicité*, and the action was fought so near the shore that the young Prince of Orange and the British and French Ambassadors were witnesses. After a distant cannonade, about noon the combatants ran alongside each other, and, ultimately, the French commander being slain and 100 of his men killed or wounded, the enemy surrendered, to the chagrin, doubtless, of the representative of France and the satisfaction of his English colleague. Captain Hood, of the *Minerva*, 32, who afterwards gained a peerage, engaged and captured in the Channel, after a protracted engagement, the *Warwick*, formerly of the British navy, armed with 36 guns. It was a brilliant feat of arms, as the enemy was greatly superior in every way to the *Minerva*, and Captain Hood displayed the pertinacity that always distinguished him ; for though during the action he lost his bowsprit and foremast, he refitted his ship, and making sail overtook and again brought the *Warwick* to action, finally compelling her to strike. Almost as meritorious was the capture of the *Entreprennant* by the *Vengeance*, Captain Nightingale, a frigate of equal force. Thrice the ships were engaged yard-arm to yard-arm, and the Frenchman escaped each time after making an attempt to board : but Captain Nightingale would not be denied, and ranging up again within pistol-shot he forced the *Entreprennant* to strike. A third action was fought in the Mediterranean between the *Oriflamme*, 40, and the *Isis*, 50, Captain Wheeler, which merits special notice. The *Isis*, having overhauled the Frenchman at six o'clock in the evening, maintained a running fight with her for over four hours, during which Captain Wheeler was killed, and then closing, boarded and captured the enemy. Two actions between ships-of-the-line also should receive brief mention here.

The *Thunderer*, 74, being off Cadiz in company with three frigates, overhauled and engaged the *Achille*, of equal force, and captured her within half an hour, during which so accurate and deadly was the *Thunderer's* fire that her adversary had 40 killed and 100 wounded.

But more remarkable was the memorable engagement between the 74 *Bellona*, Captain Faulknor (who was accompanied by the *Brilliant*, 30, Captain Logie), and the *Courageux*, in weight of metal the same, but having 150 more men, which was in company with two frigates. The ships met off the Tagus, and while Captain Logie prevented the frigates from assisting the *Courageux*, and handled his ship with as much skill as dash, the captains of the 74's, equally confident and anxious to put their mettle to the test, cleared for action. The conditions as to

wind and sea were favourable, and when the ships
approached within pistol-shot of each other the
eager crews opened fire, and a deadly cannonade
began, while from the poop, forecastle, and tops a
heavy discharge of small arms was maintained.   In
less than ten minutes all the *Bellona's* rigging was
cut to pieces, and the mizen-mast went over the
side, when the *Courageux* fell athwart-hawse her
adversary, and opened on her a raking fire.   But
Captain Faulknor, with the skill of a practised seaman and the coolness of a veteran, managed to
clear his ship, and, "wearing" round, got upon her
beam and opened so terrific a fire, pouring in a storm
of round-shot into her portholes, that the *Courageux*
in twenty minutes' time struck her colours.   The
damage the enemy sustained had reduced her to the
condition of a wreck, with only her foremast and bowsprit standing, while her sides were rent open and
her decks ploughed up by the hurricane of missiles.
Over 220 men had been killed alone, while the loss
of the *Bellona* did not exceed 40, and she had suffered little in her hull, though the rigging had been
almost entirely shot away, scarce a shroud or brace
being left.

The year 1762 was signalised by some brilliant
captures. A Spanish privateer struck to the *Milford*,
Captain Mann, who was killed, as well as his first
lieutenant, Mr. Day, who had assumed command on

D

the death of his chief; and the *Ventura* became a
prize to the *Fowey*, of equal force, whose captain,
Mead, stuck to his enemy during the night, when
she sought to fly, and, bringing her to action again
in the morning, compelled her to surrender. What
sailors would call "a great haul" was made when, off
Cape St. Vincent, two frigates captured the Spanish
Hermione, having on board 2,600,000 dollars, which
were carried in procession through the streets of
London to the Bank of England, to the admiration
of the people and the enrichment of the British
crews. The *Terpsichore* also captured a French ship
of 20 guns, and the *Brune* took the *Oiseau*, 26,
after a spirited action. During this year, the last of
the war, peace being concluded at Paris on the 10th
February following, the French lost by capture 18
ships-of-the-line and 36 frigates, and the Spaniards
12 of the former class, while the French only
captured two of our frigates.

During the American War of Independence, between 1776 and 1782, the navy had little chance of
distinguishing itself at sea, but there was severe
fighting on the inland lakes. When, however, the
French joined the insurgents, and then the Spanish
and Dutch Governments declared war against this
country, England was hard put to it on the sea, and
in 1780, for the first time since the battle of Beachy
Head, our fleets temporarily lost the command of

the sea, and experienced the indignity of witnessing a combined French and Spanish fleet sail up the Channel and threaten Plymouth. Not only this, but Gibraltar suffered a prolonged siege, and had it not been thrice relieved by Admirals Rodney, Darby, and Howe, this great fortress, the key to the Medi-- terranean, must have returned to its allegiance to Spain. Notwithstanding the odds against England, our seamen found many opportunities of showing their valour, of which we will give some instances.

On the 15th June, 1780, the *Apollo*, Captain Powell, engaged the *Stanislas*, and forced her on shore, and this engagement is chiefly memorable as being the first occasion on which Lieutenant Pellew, afterwards Lord Exmouth, came into notice, as, on the death of Captain Powell, he assumed command of the *Apollo*. Captain Williams, of the *Flora*, 36, was more fortunate, for he succeeded in capturing the *Nymphe* after a hard-fought action—a frigate which Captain Pellew commanded with such success in the Revolutionary War. When the ships fell on board each other, the Frenchmen, finding them- selves no match in gunnery for their opponents, attempted to board the *Flora*, but were driven back, and then Captain Williams, calling up his boarders, headed an attack on the enemy, and the colours of the *Nymphe* were struck, with the loss of 63 killed and 73 wounded out of 291 men, or nearly half her

crew. When Holland joined our other enemies
towards the close of 1780, Parliament voted nearly
nine millions sterling and 90,000 men for the service of the navy, and Admiral Parker, who engaged
a Dutch fleet off the Dogger Bank in July, 1781,
found them as stubborn as in the days when Blake
struggled with Van Tromp and De Ruyter for the
mastery of the Channel.

But there was a reverse side to this picture, and
our navy sustained losses at the hands of the noto-
rious American privateersman, Paul Jones. While
convoying a fleet of merchantmen, Captain Pearson,
of the 44-gun frigate *Serapis*, encountered this
officer, then in the French service, while commanding the *Bon Homme Richard*, 40, and accompanied
by the *Alliance*, 26. A desperate action ensued,
and the *Bon Homme Richard* had actually hauled
down her colours, when Paul Jones, running her
alongside the *Serapis*, suddenly boarded the British
frigate and captured her. The slaughter was almost
unprecedented, for while the *Serapis* lost 48 killed
and 68 wounded, the French cruiser, whose stern
and quarter were beaten in and most of her lower-
deck guns dismounted, had nearly 300 casualties,
and the ship actually foundered on the following
day. The court-martial that sat on Captain Pearson,
on returning him his sword, complimented him on
his gallantry, and his sovereign knighted him.

Another remarkable action, which had a sad termination, was that between the *Quebec*, 32, Captain Farmer, and the *Surveillante*, 40. Both sides fought with the utmost fury, but at length the British frigate, which had lost 80 seamen and marines killed and wounded, caught fire and blew up with the British colours still flying, when 15 officers and eight men perished. Lieutenant Roberts, one of the survivors, who was picked up by a boat, was promoted to the rank of commander, and the King conferred a baronetcy on the eldest son of the commander of the *Quebec*. Lord Nelson, when a boy, served many years under Captain Farmer, and the glorious death of his old chief must have profoundly affected one who, throughout his career, put in practice the lessons he had learnt under that heroic officer, and died no less glorious a death.

The actions between single ships in 1781 merit special notice. The *Nonsuch*, 64, Sir James Wallace, belonging to Admiral Darby's fleet, on its return from revictualling Gibraltar, brought to action the *Actif*, 74, during the night of the 14th May. Having first raked her, she ran alongside, but although the *Actif* shook her adversary off and made sail, about five o'clock in the morning Captain Wallace, having refitted, got within cannon-shot range of the Frenchman, and then discovered her superiority ; but this only inspired him with fresh resolution, and he renewed the action, though his efforts were vain, and the *Actif* escaped to Brest, the *Nonsuch* having sustained a loss of 26 killed and 64 wounded. The *Flora*, Captain Williams, and *Crescent*, Captain Hon. T. Pakenham, sighted two Dutch frigates off the Barbary coast, and after an action lasting over two hours, the former captured the *Castor*, whose casualties were 63; but Captain Pakenham was not equally successful in his action with the *Brill*, and having lost his main and mizen-masts, the *Crescent* became unmanageable, and her flag was struck, with the loss of 26 killed and 67 wounded. Captain Williams now bore down to her assistance, and the *Brill* made sail, abandoning the *Crescent*, but Captain Williams was unable to bring his hard-won prize into port or save his shattered consort, for two frigates hove in sight, and he barely succeeded in making his own escape.

A frigate action worthy of notice took place in 1782, the last year of this war, the most disastrous England had ever waged, for she lost both colonies and credit, and ceded islands in the West Indies and settlements in India to France, Minorca and Florida to Spain, and Trincomalee and other places in Ceylon to Holland. The British 36-gun frigate *Santa Margarita*, formerly of the Spanish service, chased the *Amazone*, of equal force, and having brought her to action, after a brief but well-directed cannonade, so

disabled her adversary that she surrendered, her loss
being no less than 70 killed, including her captain,
and nearly 80 wounded. Captain Salter took his
prize in tow, but, on sighting a squadron of the
enemy, was fain to cast her adrift and seek safety in
flight. In April of this year the *Foudroyant,* under
the command of Captain Jervis, while serving under
Admiral Barrington, overhauled off Brest the French
74, *Pégase,* and soon after midnight opened fire on
the enemy. So accurate was the *Foudroyant's* fire,
that within an hour the *Pégase* was forced to strike,
having lost 80 men killed and wounded, the British
loss being *nil.* There could not be a more remarkable instance of the necessity for good gunnery in
winning an action, for though the *Foudroyant* was
slightly superior to the foe, she inflicted, chiefly due
to this circumstance, a defeat similar to what she
had experienced at the hands of the little *Monmouth.*
Captain Jervis, whose ships were always the best
disciplined and drilled in the navy, received the
ribbon of the Bath for his victory, and lived to win
an earldom. Probably on the merits of the action
he was of the opinion he expressed on a subsequent
occasion regarding the capture, on the 21st April,
1798, of the *Hercule* by the *Mars,* "an old commissioned and well-practised ship," that the result of
the action was a foregone conclusion.

CHAPTER II.

WITH the war of the French Revolution began the most glorious period in the history of the British navy. Reduced gradually after the peace, the estimates for the navy in 1792 were £15,000 below two millions, and the number of men voted by Parliament had sunk to 16,000 men, but great was the enthusiasm of the nation inspired by the French declaration of war with England on the 1st February, 1793, shortly after the execution of Louis XVI. Parliament voted supplies for 40,000 seamen and 5,000 marines, and 21 additional ships-of-the-line and some frigates were ordered to be commissioned. Lord Howe, a veteran officer of the old wars and the most trusted now that Rodney was gone, was verging on three score years and ten, but with alacrity he assumed command of the Channel fleet, and put to sea on the 14th July, 1793, and on the "Glorious First of June" in the following year gained his great victory over the French fleet. But long before this our frigates had established their superiority over the enemy in those duels which were the glory of the service, and afforded our officers the best opportunity of showing what was in them. In nearly every instance all our best officers—Nelson, the two Hoods, Collingwood, Cornwallis, Pellew, Parker, Cochrane, Saumarez, and a host too numerous to specify—showed their mettle when in command of frigates by successfully engaging the enemy's ships.

The exigencies of space prevent our detailing, or even mentioning, all the actions between privateers and small craft that took place throughout the prolonged hostilities which were waged between England and France between 1793 and 1815, with the exception of the brief period in 1802, when the Treaty of Amiens gave a delusive promise of peace. But mention must be made of the first of the long series, the action on the 13th March, 1793, between the *Scourge*, of eight guns and 70 men, and the French privateer *Sans Culotte*, of 12 guns and 81 men, which struck, with the loss of nine killed and 20 wounded. We must also mention the circumstances under which the first British officer fell in the

service of his country.   A detachment of seamen from
the *Syren*, under the command of Lieutenant Western,
captured some batteries on the coast of Holland, and
a few days later, as he was in the act of laying one of
the guns against the enemy's entrenched camp, he
was killed by a musket-ball, which passed through
his head.   The Duke of York, who commanded the
British army in Holland, attended the funeral of this
gallant officer, and ordered the erection of a monument in the church of Dordrecht where he was
interred.

The 32-gun frigate *Iris*, Captain Lumsdaine, on
the 13th May, 1793, engaged the privateer *Citoyenne
Française*, until the latter made sail to escape, when,
as Captain Lumsdaine was about to pursue, his fore
and mizen-masts went over the side, and he had to
relinquish all hope of making a prize of the Frenchman, which, it was subsequently ascertained, lost her
captain and 15 officers and men killed, and 37
wounded, the total loss of the *Iris* being 36, of whom
three were officers, one, her master, being mortally
wounded.   A fortnight later the *Venus*, 32, Captain
J. Faulknor, descried the *Semillante*, 40, and after
some manœuvring the frigates came to close quarters,
and all went well for the *Venus*, which was displaying
her superiority of fire, when another French sail
hove in sight, and the British frigate, whose main
rigging was shot away and her spars and sails greatly

damaged, "hauled her wind" and sought safety in flight. She only lost two men killed, and her master and 19 seamen wounded, while the *Semillante's* loss was 12 and 20 respectively. More important was the next action we have to chronicle, but though the valour of the crew of the British ship was not less conspicuous, it was not rewarded with success. The *Hyæna*, of 24 guns and 120 men, while cruising off Cuba, was chased and brought to bay by the *Concorde*, of 40 guns and 320 men, the advanced ship of a squadron, and after "a severe and spirited conflict," Captain Schomberg, the naval historian, says, was obliged to surrender. Captain (afterwards Sir William) Hargood was tried by court-martial for the loss of his ship and honourably acquitted, the sentence being that "every means had been used to prevent the *Hyæna* from being captured."

But this surrender to a ship of greatly superior force with a French squadron coming up astern, was amply redeemed by the brilliant victory achieved by Captain Edward Pellew, afterwards Lord Exmouth, the conqueror of Algiers. At daylight on the 18th June—a date destined to be so glorious in our annals —when in command of the *Nymphe*, 36, while cruising in the Channel, he sighted the French *Cleopatre*, of slightly inferior force as regards her broadside weight of metal, but carrying 80 more men. To sight was for Captain Pellew to give chase, and at 6 A.M.

the enemy, finding that escape was impossible, or, it may be, desirous of trying conclusions with a ship of equal force, shortened sail and waited for her adversary. On nearing his foe Captain Mullon, of the *Cleopatre*, hailed the *Nymphe*, hat in hand, and Captain Pellew, not to be behindhand in politeness, doffed his headgear likewise and replied, when the crew of the British frigate gave three cheers, to which the Frenchmen replied. No time was lost, however, in exchanging compliments, and the *Nymphe* having reached a position from which her foremost guns bore on the starboard quarter of the enemy, Captain Pellew replaced his hat on his head—the preconcerted signal to open fire. The *Cleopatre* replied, and the ships, running before the wind, kept up a heavy fire within pistol-shot range until, within a quarter of an hour of the commencement of the action, the *Cleopatre* "hauled her wind," and shortly after her mizen-mast went over the side and her wheel was shot away. As a result of this she "paid off" before the wind and fell on board the *Nymphe*, her jibboom passing between the fore and main-masts of the British frigate. Soon the ships ranged alongside each other, and a few minutes after seven o'clock, within an hour of the first shot being fired, the boarders were called away by Captain Pellew, and, vaulting over the Frenchman's side, after a brief resistance hauled down the tri-coloured flag.

The *Nymphe*, out of a complement of 240 men
and boys, lost three midshipmen, a master's mate, the
boatswain, and 18 seamen and marines killed ; and
her second lieutenant, two midshipmen, one lieutenant
of marines, and 23 men wounded, the total loss thus
being 50.   The *Cleopatre*, out of 320 all told, had
63 placed *hors de combat*, among the killed being her
captain, while three of her lieutenants were wounded.
It is related of the gallant commander that when
mortally wounded, being desirous of saving the list
of coast signals from falling into the hands of the
enemy, he drew out of his pocket what he thought
was the paper, and died while in the act of biting it
to pieces, though it proved to be the commission of
the unfortunate officer.   Captain Pellew brought his
prize to Portsmouth, and a few days after his arrival
Lord Chatham introduced him to King George III.,
as well as his brother, Captain Israel Pellew, who had
accompanied him in the cruise, who commanded the
Conqueror, 74, at Trafalgar, and was almost as distinguished as his relative.   The King knighted the
commander of the *Nymphe*, and promoted his brother
to post rank.   Under the name of *Oiseau*, there being
already a *Cleopatra* in the navy, the prize was purchased into the service.

As desperate but not so fortunate in its result was
the next action we are called upon to register in our
rôle of impartial historian of defeats and victories

alike. The British 32-gun frigate *Boston*,* Captain
Courtenay, on the North American station, had for
some time been cruising off New York with the object
of intercepting the French frigate *Embuscade*, of equal
weight of metal, but carrying over 100 more men,
which had lately captured or destroyed upwards of
60 British merchantmen. Captain Bompart, mistaking her for the *Concorde*, then cruising in those seas,
sent his first lieutenant with a boat's crew to board
the stranger, with a view of giving his orders to her
commander. The skilled eye of the officer detected
something British about the ship's neatness and seamanlike look aloft, and he lay on his oars, but was
reassured as to her nationality by an American pilot,
who had been taken in by a *ruse* of Captain Courtenay's, who, to delude the Yankee when he was passing under his stern, had hoisted French colours, and
placed some of his crew abaft who spoke French, in
which language they chattered with the volubility of
that nation. On the *Embuscade's* officer boarding
the *Boston*, Captain Courtenay politely informed him
of his desire to meet his ship in single combat at any
day and hour most convenient to Captain Bompart,
just as off the port of Boston twenty years later
Captain Broke, of the *Shannon*, challenged the

---

* Ships were classed in a method not wholly intelligible to a lands-
man, and carried more guns than their rate denoted. Thus the
Boston, though called a 32-gun frigate, had 38 guns.

commander of the *Chesapeake*. The French officer
expressed his opinion that his superior would like
nothing better than to meet his foe, and accordingly
a letter was sent ashore by the pilot boat, and within
the stipulated time of three days the *Embuscade* got
under weigh and put out to sea. It was at dawn on
the 31st July that Captain Courtenay descried a ship
under all sail heading towards him, and he immediately cleared for action. Within a few minutes
after five o'clock the frigates, their crews eager to
engage, were within cannon-shot range, and the ball
was opened with a discharge from the *Boston's* port
broadside, which was promptly answered by the
Embuscade's starboard battery as she lay with her
main-topsail to the mast awaiting her adversary.
The *Boston* then " wore " and came round on the
beam of the enemy, and the action that ensued was
viewed by crowds of Americans standing on the
Jersey beach, about four leagues distant. The mis-
fortunes of the *Boston* began very early in the action,
for within a quarter of an hour of its commencement
her cross-jack yard (the lower yard on the mizen-
mast) was shot away, and soon after all her braces
and bowlines and some of her standing rigging were
cut to pieces, and she became unmanageable. Within
an hour of the first shot being fired her main-topmast
fell over the side, and about the same time Captain
Courtenay and Lieutenant Butler of the Marines were

killed by the same round shot. Other damage ensued aloft, and both the lieutenants were wounded,
but one of them, Edwards, returned to the deck and
assumed command of the ship on the death of his
chief. The *Embuscade* was enabled to take any
position she chose, and as the guns of the *Boston* on
one side were masked by the wreck of the main-
topmast, she was about to bring her fire to bear on
that side, when, the British frigate being in a crippled
state, Lieutenant Edwards decided to discontinue the
action, and, putting his ship before the wind under
what little sail he could make, abandoned the field
to his opponent, who, to all appearance, was almost
as much disabled as herself. With her third lieutenant and 12 men absent in a prize, the *Boston*
could only muster 204 men at her quarters, and
lost eight killed, besides the two officers specified,
and 24 wounded, of whom five were officers. The
Embuscade, on the other hand, went into action with
327 men, and that she did not come out of it unscathed is proved by the admission of the loss of 50
hors de combat, while all her masts had to be taken
out on her return to New York, so that the resistance made by the British frigate was in every way
very creditable to her crew.

More successful was Captain James Saumarez,
Nelson's second in command at the Nile, of the
Crescent, 36, in an action with the *Réunion*, of like

force, off Cherbourg. Captain Saumarez had received
information that this frigate and another had made it
a practice in turn to run out of port in the evening,
stand across the Channel and make what captures
they could, returning to Cherbourg the following
morning. Accordingly, on the night of the 19th
October, 1793, Captain Saumarez took his station off
Cape Barfleur to intercept the enemy, and surely
enough, as day dawned, the *Réunion* was descried in
company with a large cutter returning from her
cruise. The *Crescent* quickly overhauled the Frenchman and brought her to close action, but had the
misfortune early to lose her fore-topmast. Putting
her helm "hard-a-starboard" Captain Saumarez
brought his ship round on the opposite tack, and
opened fire with his port guns ; and as the enemy
had by this time also lost her mizen-topmast and
foreyard, matters were again placed on a footing of
equality between the combatants, and Captain Saumarez improved his chances by taking up a position
which enabled him to pour a heavy raking fire into
the *Réunion*, which compelled her to haul down her
colours. The superiority of the British crew as
gunners was incontestably proved, for whereas out of
320 officers and men on board she lost 120, the
Crescent had not a man killed by the enemy's fire,
which as usual was mostly directed at the rigging.
On the other hand, it is only fair to record that the

E

British frigate threw a far heavier broadside than her prize, though she was a smaller craft. The cutter escaped into Cherbourg with the news of the disaster, fortunate in escaping capture at the hands of the British frigate *Circe*, which came up at the close of the engagement.

The first action in which the great Nelson was engaged in the war took place on the 22nd of this month of October off the island of Sardinia, where he was cruising in the *Agamemnon*, 64, and, sighting a squadron of four frigates and a corvette, gave chase. During the running conflict with one of them the *Agamemnon* sustained so much damage aloft that they managed to make good their escape, though it is a certain thing that had the nationality of the combatants been changed, four British frigates would not have shrunk from a conflict with a small 64.

A brilliant and successful defence was made by the 32-gun frigate *Thames*, Captain Cotes, having a crew of 187 men, against a ship of vastly superior force, the *Uranie*, of 44 guns and 320 hands, and nearly double the tonnage of her adversary. The first shot was fired at 10.30, and the battle raged with great fury till 2.20 P.M., when the *Uranie*, taking up a position under the stern of the British frigate, raked her, and then attempted to board on her quarter. In this she was unsuccessful, a few well-placed shot through her bows compelling her to desist, on which the French crew made sail, which

was hailed by hearty cheers from the tars of the
Thames, though she was in too crippled a condition
to chase her pusillanimous foe. Her loss was 11
men killed and 23 wounded, including her second
lieutenant, master, one master's mate, and a midshipman. The number of casualties on board the
Uranie is not known, but it was ascertained that her
captain was killed. The *Thames* was reduced to the
condition of a wreck. All her running and standing
gear was cut to pieces, her three lower masts and
bowsprit were shot through in several places and
tottered to their fall, and the spars were so pierced
with missiles as to be mostly useless and had to be
replaced. The hull was equally shattered, and nine
shot had passed between wind and water, and almost
all the gun tackle was carried away. While in this
forlorn condition four fresh French sail hove in
sight, and when one of them ranged under the stern
and gave her a broadside she had no option but to
surrender. The *Thames* was taken to Brest, and it
was said that the officers and men were pillaged of
their effects by the crew of the *Carmagnole*, the
frigate that brought them in tow to that port.

The next action in point of date was fought off
the island of St. Domingo, between the *Penelope*, 32,
Captain Rowley, and *Inconstante*, 36, which struck
her flag, though it should be noted that this was not
done until another British frigate, the *Iphigenia*,

came on the scene. The prize, which had her captain wounded and her first lieutenant killed, was
purchased into the service. The last action of the
year 1793, though not between frigates, is worthy
of a brief mention, both for the praiseworthy conduct
of the British crew and the slaughter they inflicted
on a much superior enemy. The *Antelope*, a small
packet, commanded by Mr. Curtis, being on her way
from the West Indies to England, fell in with two
privateers, but shaking off one of them on the following day, the second, named *Atalante*, carrying
eight 3-pounders to the *Antelope's* six, ranged up
alongside the British packet and a desperate action
commenced. The crew of the privateer lashed the
vessels together and attempted to board. They
hoped their superior numbers would ensure them the
victory. But every attempt was repulsed, and at
length, finding they had " caught a Tartar," they cut
the lashing and sought to make off. But now it was
the turn of the British sailors, and the boatswain, Mr.
Pasco, who was in command, the captain having been
killed and the only other officer shot through the
body, ran aloft and lashed the rigging of the two
vessels together. Soon after the privateersmen called
for quarter, and on boarding her it was found that
out of 65 hands she had lost the captain, chief officer,
and 30 killed and 17 wounded, the casualties of the
packet being only three killed and four wounded out

of 21 men, exclusive of some passengers who took part in the affray.

Early in the ensuing year the French fitted out some frigates to cruise in squadrons in the British Channel, and great damage was inflicted on our commerce. In order to check these depredations, frigate squadrons were despatched from our shores, and one, commanded by Sir John Borlase Warren, who had his broad pennant in the *Flora*, 36, was very successful. The other ships under the Commodore's orders were the *Arethusa*, 38, Sir Edward Pellew, and the 36-gun frigates *Melampus*, Captain Wells, *Concorde*, Sir Richard Strachan, and *Nymphe*, Captain Murray. Early in the morning of the 23rd April the British squadron sighted four strange sail, which proved to be the *Pomone*, 44, the 36-gun frigates *Résolue* and *Engageante*, and the corvette *Babet*, 20. The *Flora* got into action first and received the fire of the squadron, which so cut up her rigging aloft that she fell astern, when her place was taken by the *Arethusa*, which, together with the *Melampus* and *Concorde*, quickly overhauled them, and the two former renewed the action with the *Babet* and *Pomone*. The *Babet*, being much crippled aloft, was compelled to surrender, and the *Pomone*, about an hour and a half later, after a brave resistance, being reduced to the condition of a wreck by the combined fire of the *Arethusa* and *Melampus*, had to follow her example. The other frigates continued the pursuit of the *Résolue* and *Engageante,* and soon the *Concorde* brought the latter to close action, and after a very gallant defence the crew of the Frenchman hailed to say they surrendered. The *Résolue,* after exchanging a few shot with Sir Richard Strachan, continued her flight, and as the *Melampus* and *Nymphe* were slow to overtake her, she made good her escape into port. In this action the *Nymphe,* being a bad sailer, had no share, so that there were four ships on either side, but yet the British squadron was superior in weight of metal, and the resistance made by the enemy was a creditable one. The British casualty-roll was very small, but the ships engaged suffered greatly aloft by the fire of the French, who on their part sustained heavy losses, the *Pomone* losing over 80 men and the *Babet* between 30 and 40, but the *Engageante,* their Commodore's ship, suffered still more under the *Concorde's* fire, and all her masts were shot overboard. The three prizes were added to the navy, and the *Pomone* performed good service under, her new flag until her loss not long after her capture.

In the East Indies the *Orpheus,* 32, Captain Newcome, being in company with the *Centurion,* 50, Captain Osborne, and the *Resistance,* 44, Captain Pakenham — a ship which subsequently blew up with all on board, as was supposed, from the charred wreckage found—having outsailed her consorts, brought to action the *Duguay-Trouin*, 34, formerly the *Princess Royal*, East Indiaman, which, after a protracted resistance, struck the Tricolor, having experienced a loss of 21 killed and 60 wounded, that of the *Orpheus* being only one midshipman slain and an officer and eight men wounded.

In home waters the *Swiftsure*, 74, Captain Boyles, captured the *Atalante*, 36, after a very brave resistance, which reflected great credit on her captain, Monsieur Linois. This officer, in 1801, inflicted a reverse on British arms at Algeciras, where his opponent was Admiral Saumarez, but three years later suffered a defeat at the hands of Commodore Dance from a fleet of East Indiamen, and finished his career by falling a prisoner into the hands of the English, for while on his return from the Indian Seas on the 13th March, 1806, he encountered off the Azores Sir John Warren's squadron, and, with his flagship the *Marengo*, 80, and *Belle Poule*, frigate, was captured, the gallant Linois receiving a severe wound during the brilliant defence of his ship.

The capture of the *Atalante* by the 74 was a certainty if she could only overhaul her; but the next success we have to tell was of a far more meritorious character, and Captain Laforey, of the 28-gun frigate *Carysfort*, had the further satisfaction of re-capturing a ship that had formerly flown the Union Jack. This was the *Castor*, 32, which only ten days

before, on the 19th May, 1794, had been taken by
Admiral Nielly's squadron, together with the greater
part of the merchantmen she was convoying from
Newfoundland, and her commander, Captain Thomas
Troubridge, one of the most celebrated officers of the
navy and a life-long friend of Nelson's, who was taken
prisoner, witnessed from the deck of the *Sans Pareil*,
a French 80-gun ship, the great battle of the " Glorious
First of June " between Lord Howe and Admiral
Villaret-Joyeuse. The action between the *Carysfort*
and *Castor* lasted one hour and a quarter, at the end
of which time the Frenchman had had quite enough of
it and struck her flag, with the loss of 16 killed and
nine wounded out of a complement of 200, while the
casualties of the British frigate might be numbered on
the fingers of one hand. It was a very one-sided
affair, though the superiority in crew and armament
was all on the side of the enemy, and Captain Laforey
was knighted by the King in acknowledgment of his
gallantry, while his first lieutenant, Worsley, as
customary on such occasions, was promoted to the
rank of commander.

Sir James Saumarez, commanding the *Crescent*—
who had been knighted for his capture of the *Réunion*
in the previous October—exhibited a brilliant instance
of his professional skill in the way he handled his
ship, and so saved from capture two small frigates of
the squadron under his command when chased by a

greatly superior force.   He was cruising off the island
of Guernsey, of which he was a native, when a powerful French squadron appeared in sight, and while he
kept them at bay, the Commodore directed the *Druid*
and *Eurydice* to make the best of their way into port,
and it was only by distracting the attention of the
enemy and standing along the French line, thus
drawing their fire on him, that he secured their safety,
when the experienced pilot he had on board the
Crescent brought her also into Guernsey Road by an
intricate passage never before threaded by a man-of-
war.   It was by these deeds of skill and daring, as
much as by their valour in battle, that our frigate
captains earned the reputation which made them the
dread of the enemy.

Captain the Hon. W. Paget, commanding the 50-
gun frigate *Romney*, effected the capture in the Levant
of the *Sibylle*, 40, though in this case, owing to the
superiority of the British frigate, the result was a foregone conclusion.   The *Sibylle* was at anchor in a
roadstead, and Captain Paget, anchoring within a
cable's length (240 yards) of the enemy, sent a boat
with a message to Commodore Rondeau, demanding
the surrender of his ship so as to save the useless
effusion of blood.   This the French officer declined,
on which Captain Paget warped the *Romney* abreast of
the Frenchman, with springs on her cables—lines
carried out from the stern so as to cant the ship—and

at 1 P.M. commenced the action by firing a broadside, to which the *Sibylle* replied.   For 70 minutes
the fight was hotly continued, when the enemy, being
reduced to a defenceless condition by the *Romney*'s
fire, hauled down the Republican flag.   The desperate
valour with which Commodore Rondeau conducted the
defence of his ship was proved by the fact that he lost,
out of a crew of 380, his second lieutenant, captain
of the marines, and 44 men killed and 112 wounded,
some mortally.   The *Romney* had only eight killed
and 30 wounded, but her crew, owing to her being short
of her complement, only numbered 266 all told.   Her
broadside weight of metal, according to James, always
an unimpeachable authority, was 414 pounds to 380
of the enemy, and as her crew was numerically inferior,
the odds on her side were not very great, so that the
result must be ascribed to the better gunnery of the
British crew.   The *Sibylle*, being a new ship, was
purchased into the service.

Passing over the destruction of the *Volontaire*, 36,
by Sir John Warren's squadron off the Penmarck
Rocks in the Channel, we have the capture of the
Revolutionaire by Captain Nagle, of the *Artois* (both
44-gun frigates), of the same squadron, after an
action lasting forty minutes.   It was unfortunate
that Captain Nagle was deprived of the entire credit
of his victory the proximity of the *Diamond*, and
doubtless the captain of the *Artois*, who was knighted,

deprecated the presence of his consort as much as
Captain Thévenard had cause to congratulate himself
on that lucky circumstance, by which the surrender
was robbed of the sting of disgrace. The *Revolutionaire*, under her own name, was received into the
navy, and with the *Pomone* and *Sibylle* was one of
the finest ships of her class in the service.

The last frigate action of the year we have to
chronicle is that between the *Centurion*, 50, Captain
Osborne, and *Diomede*, 44, Captain Matthew Smith,
with a French squadron, consisting of the *Cybèle*, 40,
Prudente, 36, flying the broad pennant of Commodore Renaud, *Jean Bart*, 20, and the 14-gun brig
Courier. It was off Port Louis, in Mauritius (then
called the Isle of France), that the encounter took
place, but it was of an indecisive character, and after
much cannonading, in which the *Diomede* afforded
little assistance to her consort when closely engaged
with the *Cybèle*, the French squadron escaped. This
frigate might at least have been captured, but the
Centurion, being much cut up aloft, was not in a
condition to prevent her adversary from joining the
French commodore and making good her escape, for
which Captain Smith was afterwards brought before
a court-martial, and sentenced to be cashiered. A
writer in the French *Victoires et Conquêtes* stated,
with the mendacity distinguishing the authors of that
great historical work, that two French frigates and a

brig—thus ignoring the presence of the corvette *Jean Bart*—had compelled two British " ships-of-the-line " to raise the blockade of Port Louis, though the departure of the *Centurion* and *Diomede* to repair damages gave some excuse to the latter part of their statement.   To which side victory inclined is rendered a matter of no doubt, for the French squadron made sail to escape, followed by the *Diomede ;* and while the *Centurion* had three killed and 23 wounded (the *Diomede* having sustained no loss), the *Prudente* acknowledged to having 15 killed, among them two senior lieutenants, and 20 wounded, including Commodore Renaud, and the *Cybèle* her first lieutenant and 21 seamen in the former category, and 62 in the latter.

The year 1795 opened with one of the most brilliant frigate actions that even the annals of the British Navy can show.   The hero of the victory was Captain Robert Faulknor, commanding the *Blanche*, 32, descended from an equally distinguished grandfather and father, the latter the officer who, when in command of the *Bellona*, 74, captured off Lisbon the *Courageux*, after a forty minutes' action, with a loss to the enemy of 300 men.   The action took place off Guadaloupe, in the West Indies, soon after midnight on the 4th January.   Her antagonist, the *Pique*, 36, was of superior force in armament and crew, having 80 more men, and her captain was so confident of victory that he came out of port to accept the challenge of the gallant Faulknor.

It was a few minutes before 1 A.M., on the 5th of January that the ships got to close quarters, running alongside each other under all plain sail. At the end of an hour and a half of heavy cannonading the *Blanche*, having shot ahead, "luffed" across the *Pique's* bow just as her own main and mizen-masts, which had been wounded by shot, went over the side. The ships now fouled each other, and as further fighting under sail was impossible, Captain Faulknor resolved not to let his adversary out of his clutches, and with the assistance of his second lieutenant, Mr. David Milne (one of a family of naval heroes as distinguished as his captain's), was in the act of lashing the *Pique's* bowsprit to the capstan of his own ship, when he received a musket-ball in the heart and died on the spot. The captain of the French frigate sought to put his superior numbers to use by boarding the *Blanche*, but these attempts were repulsed, and, a few minutes after Faulknor's death, the lashing parted and the vessels broke adrift, but the *Pique* crossing her enemy's stern, again fell foul of her, when the British crew succeeded in lashing her bowsprit to the stump of the *Blanche's* mainmast. Thus towing her astern, the British frigate pursued her course before the wind, every attempt on the part of the foe to cut her adrift being frustrated by the fire

of the marines, to which the enemy replied from their
tops and forecastle. In order to bring a raking fire to
bear on the *Pique's* bow, Lieutenant Watkins, who
had assumed command, directed that ports should be
made by blowing out the stern frame on either side
the upper transom beam, and this being done by
the two 12-pounders, their fire was brought to bear
through these improvised portholes, and played
havoc on the decks of the *Pique*. Soon after three
o'clock her mainmast followed the other masts over
the side, and her fire being masked by the wreck,
after sustaining without reply the *Blanche's* cannonade for two hours, some of the crew hailed to say
that they surrendered. All the boats having been
destroyed, Lieutenant Milne with a few men swam to
the prize to take possession of her, and thus was concluded one of the most desperate conflicts in the annals
of war.

But the victory was dimmed by the death of the
heroic Faulknor, whose loss, under the age of thirty,
was regarded as a national calamity, and was celebrated by a play at Drury Lane Theatre, entitled
Life and Death of Captain Faulknor. Out of 198
men and boys on board her the *Blanche* lost,
besides her commander, one midshipman and six men
killed, and one midshipman and 20 hands wounded,
while the *Pique*, out of 279, had no less than 76
officers and men killed, and 110 wounded (including

Captain Conseil mortally) — a casualty-roll which
exonerates her commander from the charge of having
surrendered his ship until honour was satisfied. Lieutenants Watkins and Milne were raised to the rank
of commander, and never was promotion better
merited.

The next action we have to register proved an
easy victory for the British crew, and as the superiority in guns and men was on our side, the credit
was proportionately lesssened. The *Lively*, 32, Captain Burlton, when cruising off Ushant, sighted three
French sail, and, giving chase, brought to action the
largest of them, which proved to be the 28-gun
frigate *Tourterelle*, commanded by Captain Montalan,
who, notwithstanding the odds against him, made a
very gallant resistance. For three hours he continued
the unequal fight, but when his three topmasts were
shot away, and the remaining spars and rigging much
cut up, the brave officer hauled down his colours.
The *Tourterelle* carried a furnace for firing red-hot
shot, with which she set fire to the *Lively's* sails, but
this did not avail her much, and out of 230 men
she had 16 killed and 25 wounded, the British
frigate having only two casualties. The other two
sail, which were French prizes, were retaken by the
Lively a few days later.

The advantage in the case of the action between
the *Astræa*, 32, Captain Lord Henry Paulet, and the

36-gun frigate *Gloire*, was all on the other side, but
the result was the same. The *Astræa* was one of a
British squadron, under the command of Admiral
Colpoys, which sighted and chased three French
frigates, but these dispersing, Lord Henry Paulet
overhauled and brought the *Gloire* to close action,
and after an hour's smart cannonade forced the
Frenchmen to haul down his colours. In achieving
this success the *Astræa* had her topmasts so severely
wounded that all three fell over the side within two
hours of the cessation of firing, but her loss was
merely nominal, while the *Gloire*, with 60 more
men, had 40 casualties—a remarkable instance of the
better training in gunnery of British sailors. Mr.
Talbot, first lieutenant of the *Astræa*, brought the
prize to Portsmouth and was made a commander.
One of her consorts, the *Gentille*, was captured by
the *Hannibal*, 74, but the other escaped.

Passing over the capture of two large armed French
store-ships, out of five that offered resistance, by the
Thetis, 36, Captain Hon. A. Cochrane, and *Hussar*,
28, Captain Beresford, and the surrender, after a
spirited engagement, of the *Courier National*, 18-gun
corvette, to the *Thorn*, 16, Captain Otway, we come
to the brilliant capture of the 40-gun frigate *Minerve*
by the *Dido*, 28, Captain Towry. Admiral Hotham,
while cruising off Toulon, having received information that the French fleet had proceeded to sea,

"THE BOWSPRIT OF THE 'MINERVE' BECAME LOCKED IN THE 'DIDO'S' MIZEN RIGGING."

despatched the *Dido* and *Lowestoft*, 32, Captain Middleton, to ascertain the fact by reconnoitring the port. As these frigates approached the harbour they saw the *Minerve* and *Artemise*, 36, issuing thence with the object of performing a like service as regarded the British fleet off Minorca. It was early on the 24th June that the French ships, finding the enemy of inferior force, decided to engage, and at 8.20, after some manœuvring, the *Minerve* opened fire on the *Dido*, which, however, made no reply until, a quarter of an hour later, she got close under the lee beam of the French frigate. After a few minutes the captain of the *Minerve*, deciding to bring matters to a climax by boarding, when his superior numbers would tell, tried to run the *Dido* on board amidships, but Captain Towry managed to avoid a direct blow, which would have sent his little ship to the bottom, and received it obliquely, when the bowsprit of the *Minerve* became locked in the *Dido's* mizen rigging. The French seamen now attempted to board, but were prevented by the pikemen on the quarter-deck and by their inability to get a footing owing to the great swell which bumped the ships together with great violence. At length the *Minerve's* bowsprit broke off, carrying with it, besides some of the French boarders, the *Dido's* mizen-mast, when, the colours having gone overboard with the gaff to which they were hoisted, the signal quartermaster, Barling, nailed

F

a Union Jack to the stump of the mast. The two ships now got clear of each other, but as the *Minerve* passed along she rubbed sides with her adversary, her lower yards tearing away the topsails of the *Dido*, which was left a wreck on her port quarter.

At this time the *Lowestoft* ranged up on the port bow of the French frigate, and opened fire at a distance of not more than a ship's length. So damaged had her masts become by the *Dido's* fire, that in less than ten minutes her foremast, and main, and mizen-masts came down ; and as her consort, the *Artemise*, in the most unaccountable way, after firing a broadside into each of the British frigates as she ran past them, made all sail to escape, the capture of the *Minerve* became certain. Captain Towry signalled to the *Lowestoft*, by spreading the flags over the quarter, for the mizen-mast and running gear had been shot away, to chase the *Artemise ;* but as Captain Middleton could not carry his mizen-topsail owing to the mizen-mast having been shot through, he was soon after signalled to return. He now took up a position on the *Minerve's* port quarter, and opened a heavy raking fire, which brought down her mizen-mast, and as soon after the *Dido*, having bent her fore and main topsails and rove fresh gear, made sail in the direction of the *Minerve*, Captain Perrée, seeing that further resistance would be useless, hailed the *Lowestoft* to say that he surrendered.

Out of 193 men with whom she commenced
the action, the *Dido* had her boatswain and five
sailors killed, and her first lieutenant and 14 men
wounded, while the *Lowestoft* had only three casualties. The *Minerve,* whose complement was 318,
lost 20 killed and wounded, including her captain among the latter, besides those who were
drowned when the bowsprit was shot away. Her
broadside weight of metal was superior to that of
both the British frigates, and had her consort rendered
the aid she was entitled to expect, the *Dido* at least
must have been captured, for when the *Minerve,*
whose tonnage was 1,000, and that of Captain
Towry's little ship under 600, struck her end-on,
carrying away her mizen-mast, nothing but the gallantry and skill of her noble commander saved her
from capture. The finest traditions of the British
Navy were exemplified in the conduct of this officer,
who, though he bore the brunt of the enemy's fire
and reduced his opponent to her helpless conditon
mainly by his own exertions, wrote in his official
report that "by Captain Middleton's good conduct
the business of the day was, in·a great measure,
brought to a fortunate issue." Messrs. Buckoll and
Horton, senior lieutenants of the British frigates,
were promoted, and the *Minerve,* which Captain
Towry commissioned under her own name within
eighteen months' time, had the distinction of carry-

ing the broad pennant of Commodore Nelson, which she bore to victory.

We will pass over with a bare mention the capture, after an hour's action, of the Dutch 36-gun frigate *Alliance*, by the *Stag*, 32, Captain York, because other British frigates, though they took no part in the action, were in the vicinity, and we will only briefly note the daring with which Captain Macnamara of the *Southampton*, 32, one of the most enterprising officers in the navy, chased and engaged a ship of superior force, the *Vestale*, 36, whose only anxiety seemed to be to escape from the pertinacious attentions of her adversary, in which she ultimately succeeded, owing to the *Southampton's* mizen-mast having gone over the side.

One of the most surprising incidents in the war, considering the respective strength of the parties engaged, was the action between the hired cutter *Rose*, Lieutenant Walker, carrying only 13 men and eight 4-pounders, and three French privateers, having combined crews of 146 men. While on his way from Leghorn to Corsica, which was then a British dependency, Lieutenant Walker sighted the privateers, and, bearing down on the largest of them, brought her to action, when, by the skilful handling of his little craft, he succeeded in firing broadsides into her on either side, on which she hailed for quarter. Making sail, he stood after one of the other privateers, which

he sunk by a well-directed broadside between wind
and water, when, the third having ecaped, Lieutenant
Walker returned to his prize, which he took in tow
and brought in safety to Bastia. The loss of the
prize was ascertained to be 13 out of 42 hands, and
the vessel he had sunk carried to the bottom all her
crew of 56, and this was effected by one British
officer and thirteen seamen !

The last captures made in 1795 were by the 32-
gun frigate *Mermaid*, Captain Warre, of the French
18-gun corvette *Republicaine*, off Grenada, in the
West Indies, after a running fight and close action of
ten minutes, and of the brig *Eveillé*, 16, near Rochefort, by a British squadron, including the *Pomone*,
Commodore Sir John Warren, which took possession
of her Before the year closed British expeditions
had captured from Holland the Cape of Good Hope
and her possessions in the island of Ceylon, including the important harbour of Trincomalee, also
Malacca, Chinsurah, Cochin, and all the Dutch possessions in India ; and though some of these conquests were surrendered at the Peace of Amiens, they
were re-conquered, and have ever since remained
integral portions of that Empire on which the sun
never sets.

CHAPTER III.

ONE of the most enterprising officers of our navy was Sir Sidney Smith, at this time commanding the 38-gun frigate *Diamond,* which became the terror of the French littoral. Early in 1796 Sir Sidney, with two small vessels, the *Liberty* and *Aristocrat,* stood for the port of Herqui, on the coast of France, and engaging the batteries, the guns of which he spiked, set fire to the *Etourdie,* corvette, and five smaller vessels. But Sir Sidney Smith suffered a little later for his too great temerity. On the 18th April the *Diamond* anchored in the outer roadstead of Havre, where he found the *Vengeur,* a noted privateer, carry-

ing 10 guns and 45 men, which had long preyed on
British commerce, and whose capture he determined
now to make an effort to effect.   Accordingly, with
the launch mounting an 18-pounder carronade and
four smaller boats, having 52 officers and men on
board, he proceeded in person to cut out the privateer, there being no lieutenant available to command the party, as one had left for England and the
other was ill, while the master he left in command of
the frigate.   Pushing off at 10 P.M., Sir Sidney made
a wide detour, and, as if coming from the shore,
made a dash with his flotilla, but found the lugger
fully prepared to meet him as she opened fire when
the boats were within half pistol-shot; but soon he
was alongside the *Vengeur*, which surrendered after
a brief struggle.

But now the difficulties of the enterprise were
manifest, for the crew having cut the cable, she
began drifting with the tide towards the shore.   In
vain the boats tried to tow the privateer, which at
length brought up abreast of Harfleur and nearly two
miles higher up the river than Havre.   Sir Sidney
quitted the prize for his ship, but, on observing
several boats coming out of Havre to attempt her
recapture, returned to assist in her defence, palpably
a desperate task, with all the resources of a large
town and teeming population against him.   First
sending his prisoners on *parôle* to Honfleur, on the

southern shore of the river, opposite Harfleur, he
made what scanty preparations he could for defence,
but his limited resources had been still further reduced by the return of the launch, which carried the
prisoners ashore to the *Diamond.* A large lugger
first advanced to the attack, but the *Vengeur,* which
he had got under weigh, beat her off, when many
small craft filled with troops surrounded her, and as
the breeze had completely died away, after a gallant
defence against superior numbers, Sir Sidney Smith
was compelled to surrender, having lost four killed
and seven wounded. The survivors, numbering
between 20 and 30 men, were marched to Rouen,
where they were imprisoned; but Sir Sidney and a
midshipman named Wright on the following day
were removed to Paris, where they were confined in
the Temple prison for two years, when they effected
their escape, by the connivance, it was thought, of
the French Government, who little knew when they
did this that in the British post-captain they liberated
the officer who would check Buonaparte at Acre in
his victorious career in the East, and, as he bitterly
exclaimed, rob him of his destiny. As for Mr.
Wright, he lived to fall again into the hands of the
enemy, and on the second occasion never came out
of his prison alive.

The armed store-ship *Etoile,* 28, surrendered to
the *Galatea,* 32, Captain Goodwin Keats, one of a

squadron of four frigates under command of Sir John Warren, but the four French frigates and one corvette accompanying her, after exchanging shots with the British squadron, made sail, and together with their convoy of nearly 60 ships, managed to bring to an anchor under the protection of some shore batteries. Another squadron of five frigates cruising off Ushant under command of Sir Edward Pellew, sighted the 36-gun frigate *Unité*, which was chased by the *Revolutionaire*, 38, Captain Cole, and after a brief action struck her colours ; but as the British frigate was superior in every respect and her consorts were coming up astern, there was little credit attaching to the achievement. This was the second occasion on which Captain Linois, commanding the *Unité*, fell into British hands, for in the year 1794 he was made a prisoner by the *Swiftsure*, 74, when she captured the 36-gun frigate *Atalante* after a very gallant resistance, and it was destined not to be the last.

Pellew had scarcely sent the *Revolutionaire* and her prize to Portsmouth when he sighted a strange sail, to which he gave chase with three ships, but she shook off her pursuers with the exception of the *Indefatigable*, 44, which, after a run of 168 miles, carried on for 15 hours, overhauled the enemy, which proved to be the *Virginie*. An action ensued which lasted an hour and three-quarters, both ships being under a crowd of sail, and they suffered greatly aloft, the *Virginie* losing her mizen-mast and main-top-mast, and the *Indefatigable* her gaff and mizen-top-mast; but while in this crippled condition the *Concorde* came upon the scene, thus robbing her consort of the honours she had well earned, for the French 40-gun frigate struck her colours, though had the *Concorde* not arrived the result would have been the same. Captain Bergeret made a gallant defence, and it is only just to add that the size and armament of his ship were greatly inferior to that of Sir Edward Pellew's.

The boats of the *Niger* made a gallant capture of a French lugger, having on board 105 men, which ran for shelter among the rocks off the Penmarcks, near Brest. Lieutenants Long and Thompson carried the lugger by boarding, after an obstinate resistance with small loss, when they set her on fire. The sloop-of-war *Spencer*, Captain Evans, captured after a spirited action the *Volcan*, 12-gun brig; and a few days later, off the Texel, the 36-gun frigate *Phœnix*, Captain Halsted, one of a squadron, over-took and brought to close action the Dutch frigate *Argo*, of like force, which made a good defence until, having sustained much damage aloft by the accurate fire of the British frigate and the other ships coming up astern, she surrendered to the *Phœnix*. We will only record the capture of the corvette *Revanche* by the 14-gun British brig *Suffisante*, Captain Tomlinson, after a close engagement amidst the rocks between the Cape of Ushant and the mainland, in which Tomlinson, who had obtained his promotion to the rank of commander by previous good service, again displayed his skill and daring off a lee shore on a dangerous coast.

Captain Byam Martin, of the 36-gun frigate *Santa Margarita*, achieved a commendable victory over a ship of like force, the *Tamise*, formerly the *Thames*, which, nearly three years before, had surrendered to a French squadron, after having repulsed the *Uranie*, of greatly superior size and armament. The *Santa Margarita* was accompanied by the *Unicorn*, 32, Captain Williams, and the *Tamise* by the *Tribune*, 36, and *Légère*, 18-gun corvette; but as they made sail chase was given by the British frigates, and at length Captain Martin got alongside the *Tamise*, which he compelled to strike. Though smaller, she was superior in crew and slightly in weight of metal to her opponent, and the victory was creditable to one of the best officers in our navy, who inflicted a loss on the enemy of 32 killed and 19 wounded, himself escaping almost scot-free.

Meanwhile his consort, the *Unicorn*, was not less actively engaged and with equal success. For ten hours Captain Williams maintained a running fight with his opponent, the *Tribune*, Commodore Moul-

ston (stated to be a citizen of the United States), but
the wind falling light and the enemy being cut up
aloft by her fire, the British frigate, at 10.30 P.M. on
a pleasant June night, ranged up alongside the fugitive, a much-desired event which her crew saluted
with the customary "three cheers" in which British
sailors indulge when excited by the prospect or com-
pletion of victory.   For over half an hour the ships
were closely engaged, and at length, when the smoke
cleared sway, the *Tribune* was seen attempting to
escape ; but Captain Williams overtook and renewed
the engagement, and after his fore and main-masts
and mizen-topmasts were shot away, seeing the futility
of further resistance, Commodore Moulston hauled
down his colours.   The British frigate, though of
smaller tonnage and with 100 less men, threw a
considerably heavier broadside, but, nevertheless, it
is a singular circumstance that while the *Unicorn*
had no casualties whatever, the *Tibune* lost 37 killed
and 14, including her commander, wounded. Captain
Williams was knighted, and his first lieutenant,
Palmer, and that of the *Santa Margarita*, Harrison,
were promoted.

The *Proserpine*, 40, which had sailed from Brest
in company with the captured frigates a few days
before, was sighted by the 36-gun frigate *Dryad*,
Captain Lord Amelius Beauclerk, and endeavoured to
escape, but the *Dryad* gave chase, and having gained

a position on the lee quarter, compelled her to engage
at close quarters and soon to strike her flag. The
Dryad had a slight superiority in armament, though
as usual the advantage in crew was on the side of
the enemy, the respective numbers being 254 and
346, of whom 30 were killed and 45 wounded.
The *Légére* was soon afterwards captured, and thus
the whole of the French squadron fell into British
hands and cruised under our flag, the corvette under
her own name, the *Tamise* as the *Thames* once more,
and the *Proserpine*, there being one of this name in
the service, as the *Amelia*.

A dashing achievement was performed by Captain
Macnamara, of the *Southampton*, 32, in Hyères roads,
when, under the eyes of the French gunners in Fort
Bregançon, he ran his ship athwart-hawse the *Utile*,
24, and lashing her bowsprit to his main rigging,
threw his boarders, under Lieutenant Lydiard, on the
corvette's deck, who carried her after a brief resistance, during which the gallant French commander,
Vega, and seven men were killed and 17 wounded.
Making sail on the prize, Captain Macnamara carried
her out of gun-shot of the batteries, which had opened
fire on her, and rejoined the fleet of Sir John Jervis,
who had commissioned him to undertake the difficult
task.

Equally remarkable was the feat achieved by
Captain Trollope—of the *Glatton*, of 56 guns and

350 men, a converted Indiaman—who, while seeking
to join Admiral Duncan's fleet in the North Sea,
engaged a squadron of four frigates and two corvettes. Captain Trollope was rejoiced at the
opportunity thus afforded of testing 28 68-pounder
carronades he had mounted on his main-deck, though
as the *Glatton's* ports were very small these guns
could not be traversed, and it was only possible to
point them right abeam. The enemy, confident in
their numbers, awaited him in line of battle, and the
action commenced at 10 P.M. by Captain Trollope
pouring into the commodore a broadside at 20 yards'
range, and on the van ship arriving within hail on the
other beam, the *Glatton* poured a like storm of shot
into her from his port battery, when she passed on,
leaving the British frigate engaged with the commodore on her lee-bow, another ship on her lee-beam,
and the three smaller vessels on her lee quarter.
Within an hour all firing ceased, and the enemy's
squadron withdrew to Flushing, though the dis-
mantled state of the *Glatton* rendered pursuit impossible, as nearly all the standing and running rigging
had been shot away, not a brace, and only the mizen-
stay, remaining.

Captain Mainwaring, of the *Aimable*, 32, was much
to be commiserated in finding in the French 36-gun
frigate *Pensée* a pusillanimous foe, for though at one
time, after a long running fight, the Frenchman lay

to as if for the purpose of meeting his opponent, yet,
after exchanging broadsides for a short time, the
captain of the *Pensée* seemed to be of the opinion
of Hudibras—that it was better to fly and fight
another day than stand ; and making sail he made
good his escape.   It appeared on her arrival at St.
Thomas, in the West Indies—for the action took
place off Guadaloupe, where she was blockaded—that
her loss in this indecisive action was no less than 90.
The *Mermaid,* 32, Captain Otway, off the same island,
maintained a gallant fight against the *Vengeance,*
classed as a 40-gun frigate, but carrying 52 guns.
Notwithstanding the disparity of force, Captain
Otway closely engaged the enemy, who ran under
the batteries of Basse-terre, with the loss, as stated,
of 12 killed and 26 wounded.   A fortnight later the
French frigate encountered the *Raison,* 20, Captain
Beresford, who, notwithstanding that his ship only
measured 472 tons to 1,180, the tonnage of the enemy,
with an armament and crew of proportionate strength,
did not hesitate to reply by a broadside when sum-
moned to surrender by his gigantic opponent.   After
a running fight the *Raison* outsailed the *Vengeance,*
which was lost to sight astern in a dense fog.

Equally gallant were the efforts to protect his
convoy made by Captain John Cooke—who fell at
Trafalgar when in command of the *Bellerophon*—
commanding the *Quebec,* 32, when attacked by two

French frigates; but unhappily he was not successful in saving the merchantmen, though he exchanged broadsides with one of the enemy's frigates, so as to give them an opportunity to disperse. We will only chronicle the destruction, off the Gironde, of the French frigate *Andromaque*, by the boats of the *Galatea*, Captain Goodwin Keats, and of the *Artois*, Sir Edmund Nagle, and *Sylph*, Captain White; and also the surrender of the *Elizabeth*, 36, to the *Topaze*, Captain Church, of like force, in presence of a British squadron.

The Republican Government in March, 1796, despatched a squadron to the East Indies, to carry 800 troops and supplies to the Isle of France and Bourbon (now known as Mauritius and Réunion) and harass British commerce in the Indian and Chinese seas. Rear-Admiral Sercey sailed from Rochefort with the 44-gun frigate *Forte*, carrying his flag; the *Régénérée*, 36, Captain Willaumez; *Seine*, 40; and two smaller vessels, but one of these, the *Bonne Citoyenne*, 20-gun corvette, was captured by a British squadron within a week of sailing from France, and the *Mutine*, 16, soon shared her fate—a small craft, which Nelson's Hardy commanded at the battle of the Nile. At Madeira Admiral Sercey was joined by the 40-gun frigate *Vertu*, Captain Hermite, and entered Port Louis, where he was joined by the *Prudente* and *Cybèle*, which had been blockaded there by a British squadron, thus having six frigates under his command, with which he steered for the Bay of Bengal, and thence proceeded to Sumatra, capturing some prizes on the way. Here they found themselves confronted by the Seventy-fours *Arrogant*, Captain Lucas, and *Victorious*, Captain Clark ; and an action ensued, in which, owing to the wind falling light, the British ships-of-the-line suffered considerably aloft, and so the enemy, though superior in armament and crew, which were in the proportion of two to one, were enabled to make good their escape. In this indecisive affair the *Arrogant*, out of 584 men, had one midshipman and six seamen killed, and 27 wounded, and the *Victorious*, which out of the same complement had sent away her first lieutenant and 90 hands in prizes, lost 17 killed, and her captain, a midshipman, and 53 men wounded. Admiral Sercey's squadron had not suffered equally in hull and rigging, but their united loss was 42 killed and 104 wounded. The *Arrogant* and *Victorious*, the latter in tow, made the best of their way to Madras, and Admiral Sercey steered for Batavia to repair damages.

Nothing more gallant occurred in the war than the successful resistance made by the 18-gun brig *Pelican*, Captain Searle, having only 97 men on board, against the *Medée*, mounting 40 guns with 300 men. Captain Searle, instead of attempting to escape, in which there would have been no disgrace, considering the disparity

G

of force, harangued his crew, who at first demurred to
fight, and, having succeeded in gaining their acquies-
cence, awaited his adversary, whom he beat off.
This took place in the West Indies ; while off Carthagena, in Spain, a still more celebrated officer, Captain
Bowen—a special favourite of Nelson's, who fell in
his unsuccessful attempt at Teneriffe, the only failure
of his lordship's career—of the 32-gun frigate
Terpsichore, engaged the *Mahonessa*, carrying 34
guns and 275 men, the complement of the little
Terpsichore being only 182.   The Spaniards fired a
gun as though to ascertain if there was any fight in
the " Little Devil," as they afterwards named the
British frigate, from the success and daring with
which she harassed their commerce, and Captain
Bowen replied with a broadside, and followed it up
so well that, at the end of an hour and twenty
minutes, his opponent tried to make off, trusting
to the damaged condition aloft of the *Terpsichore ;*
but in this she was frustrated, for the British tars,
with the wonderful smartness and resource for which
they were as remarkable as their gallantry in action,
had refitted the frigate and bent fresh sails within
twenty minutes, and were soon alongside the enemy,
ready to renew the action.   The *Mahonessa*, which
was equally crippled aloft, now hauled down her
colours, having lost 30 killed and the same number
wounded.

Captain Bowen, having repaired damages at Gibraltar, on the 12th December, just two months after taking the *Mahonessa*, descried off Cadiz a frigate-built ship, to which he gave chase, spreading as much canvas as his ship could carry in the gale then blowing. The stranger proved to be the *Vestale*, 36, Captain Foucaud, who had parted company with Admiral Villeneuve's fleet while on its way from Toulon to Brest, and now, making sail, appeared resolute on adopting the policy of avoiding an action, according to the custom which obtained in the French navy as regards their fleets and line-of-battle-ships, and which extended even to their frigates. A French naval writer, in *Victoires et Conquêtes*, describes these principles in the following passage :—" In the weak state of the French marine the greatest of all follies is to send ships to sea to seek and offer battle to those of the enemy. It was done, however, at the commencement of the war, and we have witnessed the ill consequences arising from it. The true policy is to deceive the vigilance of the stronger party, escape his pursuit, strike unawares upon a point which he has left unprotected. In naval matters an engagement is not always the aim to be proposed. The important point to the State is that a naval commander should execute the mission with which he is charged, and not neglect to do so in order to afford a proof of his courage and acquire a trophiless glory for his country. According to these principles, the different Governments which succeeded each other in France during the war of the Revolution have almost all of them, and very wisely, given a formal order to their flag-captains and captains to avoid an action, except in case of absolute necessity, and to devote the whole of their energies towards the accomplishment of their mission."

Truth to say, this "mission" is not a very glorious one for the great French nation, which at this time was striving to enforce its claim of universal dominion; but there was wisdom in it, and experience had shown its necessity already in Lord Howe's action of the "Glorious First of June," and a still more conclusive proof of its sagacity was afforded when Villeneuve, issuing out of Cadiz with the combined French and Spanish fleets, received his crushing defeat at Trafalgar. It is more than probable that in future hostilities the navy of France will adopt the same principles of warfare, even if reinforced by the Russian marine, unless with her possible ally, or allies, she could command superiority on the seas, which would mean for England the ruin of her commerce and loss of colonies, if not of liberty itself. But in our digression we have wandered far from our subject—the action between the *Terpsichore* and *Vestale.*

After a chase lasting all day, during which the *Terpsichore*, carrying a press of sail, sprang her fore and main-topmasts, the captain of the *Vestale* at length, when nearing the port of Cadiz, as though ashamed of his want of enterprise, hove to and awaited his adversary. The first shot was fired at 10 P.M., a very common hour apparently for the commencement of these frigate duels, as most of the more important ones—such, for instance, as the *Blanche* and *Pique*, and *Forte* and *Sibylle*—were fought at night. A spirited action ensued, but Captain Bowen had trained his men to perfection at the great guns, and at twenty minutes before twelve the *Vestale*, with her three masts and bowsprit tottering to their fall, hauled down her colours and became the prize of the *Terpsichore*, which, out of 166 men—six officers and 40 sailors being away in prizes—had four killed, and her only lieutenant on board, a brother of the captain's, and 17 men wounded. The *Vestale* began the action with 300, or, as some accounts say, with 270 hands, of whom she lost 30 killed, including her commander, and 37 wounded, among them being the first lieutenant. That the enemy did not surrender till they had done their best was proved by her damaged condition, and just as the boat of the British frigate came alongside to take possession, her masts and bowsprit fell into the sea. The scene of the contest was off Cape

Trafalgar, where nine years later the fate of England,
and, we may almost say, of Europe, was decided;
and in the excitement of the fight the ships had
drifted among the shoals off the land, and in their
shattered condition were both in great danger.
However, what cannot discipline and seamanlike
skill effect? and the master of the *Terpsichore*, who
had been placed in charge of the prize, managed to
anchor the ship, though after vain attempts to tow
her off. Captain Bowen had to put to sea when
darkness came on, and on returning the following
morning to pick his prize up again, found the *Vestale*
under jury-rig making her way to Cadiz, the crew
having overpowered the handful of Englishmen
placed on board, and, towed by some Spanish boats,
she was safely moored in port. Captain Bowen
wrote demanding her surrender, according to the
usages of war, but no notice was taken of his letter,
and he had to content himself with the barren
glory of having conquered an enemy of at least
equal force, while by some strange and unpardon-
able omission he never received the honour of
knighthood for his double victory over her and the
Mahonessa, which had been awarded in far less
meritorious instances, though his countrymen recognised his deserts, and the merchants of London
presented him with some plate—an honour conferred
shortly before on Captain Trollope, of the *Glatton*.

In the Channel took place the capture of the
privateer *Buonaparte*, of 16 guns and 137 men, by
Captain Byam Martin, of the *Santa Margarita ;* and
off Anguilla, in the West Indies, of the 20-gun ship
Decius by the *Lapwing*, 28, Captain Barton, the
enemy losing, out of 336 men on board, including a
large body of troops, no less than 80 killed and 40
wounded ; but unfortunately, while towing his prize
to St. Kitts, Captain Barton was chased by the
French frigates *Thetis* and *Pensée*, when, removing
her crew and provisions, he set fire to the *Decius*
to prevent her falling into the hands of the enemy.

The last frigate action of the year 1796 was fought
by Commodore Nelson, who had his broad pennant
flying on board the 38-gun frigate *Minerve*, Captain
George Cockburn, captured in the preceding year by
the gallant Captain Towry, of the *Dido*. The *Minerve*
was accompanied by the *Blanche*, 32, Captain Preston, another historic ship, being the one which took
the *Pique* on the 4th January, 1795, when Captain
Faulknor met his glorious death. On the 19th
December two Spanish frigates were sighted, and
while, agreeably to order, Captain Preston stood to
leeward to attack one ship, the Commodore brought
to action the larger frigate, which proved to be the
Sabina, Captain Jacobo Stewart, of 40 guns and 286
men, so that the combatants were well matched, the
crew of the British frigate numbering the same to a

man. Captain Stewart, a descendant of the exiled
royal family of England, made a gallant and protracted resistance of two hours and fifty minutes, but,
after losing 146 men, according to Nelson's despatch,
struck his colours. Meanwhile the *Blanche* engaged
the *Ceres*, and, after a feeble resistance on her part,
forced her to surrender, but Captain Preston had to
be content with a barren triumph. Lieutenants
Culverhouse and Thomas Masterman Hardy (the
captain of the *Victory* at Trafalgar), with a prize
crew of 40 men, having been placed on board the
Sabina, Nelson took her in tow, as she had lost her
mizen-mast, and the fore and main-masts were shot
through and could only carry reduced sail. But
presently another Spanish frigate was sighted, which
proved to be the *Matilda*, 34, towards which Nelson
stood, and would in all probability have captured her
as she hauled off, when a Spanish ship-of-the-line
and two frigates hove in sight, and even Nelson
considered the odds so hopeless that he made good
his escape, favoured by the darkness. The *Sabina*,
in her crippled condition, had no chance of escape,
and Lieutenant Culverhouse, when her masts had
gone over the side, surrendered to overwhelming
force.

At this time the superiority of the French and
Spanish fleets in the Mediterranean was so great that
it was resolved to abandon its waters for the present;

and Nelson, on his arrival at Porto Ferrajo, embarked
the troops and stores, and, accompanied by the
Romulus, Southampton, and *Dido* frigates, two store-
ships, and twelve transports, set sail on the 27th
January, 1797, and, after reconnoitring Toulon,
the commodore arrived at Gibraltar. Thus the
British flag was now only shown at Malta ; but Sir
John Jervis's victory over the Spanish fleet on St.
Valentine's Day, in which Nelson, who had shifted
his pennant into the *Captain,* played a prominent
part, so crippled the Spanish navy that very soon
the British fleet re-established its ascendency in the
Mediterranean, which had remained unquestioned
in the Channel, Atlantic, and North Sea, where
Duncan achieved a crushing defeat over the Dutch
navy. In the West Indies, before the close of the
year 1796, our combined fleet and army had captured
Demerara, St. Vincent, and Grenada, and retaken
Saint Lucia ; and in the East Indies Colombo, in
Ceylon, was won, and the Dutch settlements of
Amboyna and Banda in the Moluccas, together with
vast stores of merchandise and spice, each of the
five captains present receiving as his share of the
booty about £15,000 ; while in Saldanha Bay, in
Cape Colony, a Dutch fleet of nine sail was fain to
surrender without firing a shot to a superior British
fleet. Thus everywhere the flag of England was
triumphant on the sea, and under such auspices

dawned the year 1797, enriched with the glories of
St. Vincent and Camperdown.

The French Directory having decided on the
invasion of Ireland—where General Hoche (with
whom were Generals Grouchy and Humbert) was to
land in Bantry Bay—on the 16th December, 1796,
Admiral Morard-de-Galles sailed from Brest with
17 ships of-the-line and 19 frigates and corvettes,
besides transports, conveying an army of 18,000
men. The departure was witnessed by a British
frigate squadron, consisting of the *Indefatigable*,
44, Sir Edward Pellew ; *Revolutionaire*, Captain Cole ; and the 36-gun frigates *Amazon* and
Phœbe, Captains Reynolds and Barlow. The French
fleet began badly, losing the first night a 74, with
680 men out of 1,300 men on board, and, owing
to stormy winds, the ships were dispersed, and
Admiral Bouvet returned to Brest with six ships-of-
the-line, while others made for Rochefort. Even
those vessels that reached Bantry Bay, and others
that appeared off the Shannon, quitted the coast of
Ireland, and all at length steered for France, while
some of the transports and frigates were lost or
captured.

A terrible fate overtook the *Droits-de-l'Homme*,
74, Commodore la Crosse, with General Humbert on
board. While making for Belleisle, on the 13th
January, 1797, she found her passage barred by the

ACTION BETWEEN THE "INDEFATIGABLE," "AMAZON" AND "DROITS DE L'HOMME."

NOTE.—The Droits de l'Homme lost her fore and maintop masts in a squall shortly before the commencement of the action.

Indefatigable and *Amazon*, when a running fight ensued amid hazy weather, with a heavy sea, and a wind gradually increasing to a gale, so that the 74 had to keep her lower-deck ports closed. At length the frigates stationed themselves one on either bow of the *Droits-de-l'Homme*, and raked her by turns, while Commodore la Crosse, by yawing first on one tack and then on the other, managed to return their fire. This went on between 5.30 and 10.30 P.M., when her mizen-mast was cut away, as it was in a tottering state, and the frigates took post on either quarter ; but though her loss was considerable, she had a practically inexhaustible number of fighting men on board, there being 1,350, including the troops. Suddenly land appeared, when the three combatants endeavoured to haul off to avert the shipwreck that appeared imminent, and the contest, which had lasted (allowing an hour and a half's intermission while the frigates repaired damages) continuously for ten hours, was discontinued, and the struggle with the elements, which had become fiercer as the sea and wind continued to rise, demanded all their energies to avert a fearful fate. The British seamen had been fighting on the main-deck with the water up to their middles, and when the firing ceased they were completely exhausted, while there were three feet of water in the *Amazon's* hold, and four in that of the *Indefatigable*, and their masts, moreover,

were so wounded with shot as to be in danger of
going over the side.

During the action the *Droits-de-l'Homme* had lost
103 killed and 150 wounded, but the majority of
the survivors encountered a doom as terrible as their
fallen comrades.   The ship now lost her foremast
and bowsprit, and as only the mainmast was left
standing she drifted helplessly on to a bank of sand
in the Bay of Audierne ; and as she struck her sole
remaining mast went over the side, and the sea
broke over the 74, when a scene of indescribable
horror ensued, as 1,200 human beings found themselves close to the land, but unable to reach its
shelter, while as daylight broke crowds on shore
gathered to watch the ship break up and the sea
engulf their gallant countrymen ! So the day passed,
but hope of rescue there was none, and night again
closed in ; and yet another day passed, the people
being without food and water, and attempts to land
at low water were successful in but few instances,
while the boats and rafts were stove in or swamped.
On the fourth day the weather moderated, when a
vessel appeared in the offing, which managed to save
150 of the survivors ; but yet another night of
misery remained for the mariners crowding the
wreck, some 380, of whom, says Lieutenant Pipon,
a British officer, a prisoner on board, "above one-
half were found dead next morning." He adds : " I

was saved at about 10 A M. on the 18th January, with my two brother officers, the captain of the ship, and General Humbert. I fell on the locker in a kind of trance for nearly thirty hours, and was swelled to that degree as to require medical aid to restore my decayed faculties." Thus at least 1,100 souls perished in a scene which for prolonged horror and misery of battle and shipwreck is unsurpassed in the tale of the sea.

Meanwhile the *Indefatigable* and *Amazon*, making what sail they could carry, " clawed " off the land and escaped. Of the 44 sail forming the French armament that sailed from Brest, seven were captured, two ships-of-the-line and two frigates were wrecked, and two other ships foundered.

Early in the year 1797 Captain Mansfield, of the *Andromache*, 32, mistaking an Algerine frigate he overhauled for a Spaniard, closely engaged her for forty minutes, and after repulsing a determined attempt to board compelled her to surrender with the loss of 66 killed and a like number wounded. The French Government having despatched the 40-gun frigates *Resistance* and *Vengeance* and corvette *Constance*, 22, with 1,200 galley-slaves, to effect a landing on the Welsh coast, these men dressed like soldiers were disembarked in Fisgard Bay, but they were surrounded by the militia and had to lay down their arms, and so ended this futile and meaningless expedition. The

British 36-gun frigates, *San Fiorenzo*, Sir Harry
Neale, and *Nymphe*, Captain Cooke, while off Ushant
on their return to Lord Bridport's fleet after having
reconnoitred Brest, encountered the *Resistance* and
Constance, which, after a brief defence, struck their
colours, with the loss of 28 killed and 23 wounded.
The *Resistance*, re-named the *Fisgard*, was purchased
into the navy, and in October of the following year
fought a brilliant action under her new flag, which
has rendered famous her name and that of her gallant
captain, Byam Martin, already mentioned in these
pages.

While the *Immortalité* was returning to Brest
from the second abortive invasion of Ireland the
Fisgard sighted and brought her to action ; but
so well directed was the fire of the enemy, which
as usual was aimed aloft, that, having cut away the
whole of the *Fisgard's* running rigging, she made sail
to escape, but the crew of the British frigate, en-
couraged by their commander, so exerted themselves
to refit their ship that they were soon again alongside
the *Immortalité*, which, when she was in an almost
sinking state, with her mizen-mast gone by the board
and all her masts and spars much cut up, struck the
tri-colour.   Out of 580 men, including soldiers, she
lost her captain, first lieutenant, General Monge,
seven other officers, and 54 men killed and 61 of all
ranks wounded. The *Fisgard*, besides having six feet

of water in the hold and being much cut up aloft and in her hull, had, out of a complement of 281, ten killed and 26 wounded. It was a brilliant victory, as the broadside weight of metal was slightly in favour of the French frigate, while her crew, including the soldiers, who doubtless lent a hand in working the guns, were twice as numerous. The prize, like her conqueror, rendered good service to her adopted country, and we trust their names will ever appear on the Navy List as proud mementoes of two memorable victories. Among captures made during the year were a Spanish 10-gun brig privateer by the British 14-gun cutter *Viper*, Lieutenant Pengelley, after a smart action, and of the French privateer *Hardi*, carrying 18 guns and 130 men, and *Musette*, 22 guns and 150 hands, by the 18-gun sloop-of-war *Hazard*, Captain Ruddach; also of the Spanish frigates *Ninfa* and *Santa Elena*, each mounting 34 guns, with a complement of 320 men, by the *Irresistible*, 74, Captain George Martin, and *Emerald*, 36, Captain Berkeley, which were taken near Cape Trafalgar, where they had run for protection in their passage from Havana to Cadiz. The *Ninfa* was taken into the service under the name of *Hamadryad*, but the other prize foundered.

Sir John Warren's frigate squadron drove on shore the French 28-gun frigate *Calliope*, which was cannonaded by the 18-gun brig *Sylph*, and went to pieces, and her convoy were also burnt, while Captain

White of the *Sylph* rendered good service in destroying a corvette ; and the *Arethusa*, 38, Captain Wolley, took after a brief resistance the *Gaieté*, 20-gun corvette. In the West Indies the *Alexandrian*, 6-gun schooner, Lieutenant Senhouse, captured after a spirited action two French privateers of equal force, having stronger crews. The *Penguin*, 16, Captain Pulling, chased two vessels and compelled them both in succession to surrender, the larger being the privateer *Oiseau*, of 18 guns, and the other the *Empress*, of Dartmouth, her prize, formerly a French 14-gun privateer. It was a meritorious success, as, owing to a heavy breeze and the press of sail she carried, the *Penguin's* guns were knee-deep in water. Off the island of St. Domingo the *Pelican*, 18-gun brig, Lieutenant White in command in the absence of her captain ill on shore, brought to action the privateer *Trompeur*, of 12 guns and 78 men, and though she made all sail to escape, he followed her up after repairing damages, and a second time engaged her until she caught fire and blew up abaft, then going down head foremost.

Off Bayonne the *Indefatigable* recaptured the *Hyæna*, which had been taken in May, 1793, by the 40-gun frigate *Concorde*, as before related. The *Cerberus*, 32, Captain Drew, also made a prize of the privateer *Epervier*, of 16 guns and 145 men, together with a ship she had taken, and two days later captured

the 18-gun privateer *Renard,* having a complement
of 189 hands.

One of the finest officers of the navy in the war
was Captain Robert Barlow, of the 36-gun frigate
Phœbe, and he exhibited his gallantry for the first, but
not by any means for the last, time in the capture on
the night of the 20th December of the *Nereide*—a ship
of slightly less force in guns, but carrying 70 more
men.   The chase continued during the day, but at
nine o'clock, when the *Phœbe* had drawn up to the
enemy, firing commenced on both sides.   Having
cut up the rigging of the British frigate, the *Nereide*
tacked and, crowding all sail, tried to escape in the
darkness ; but Barlow also put his ship about, and
following in pursuit, at 10 P.M., got alongside
the Frenchman, who, seeing escape was impossible
with so persistent a foe, backed his main topsail, and
submitting to the inevitable resolved to fight it out.
Soon the *Nereide* fell on board the *Phœbe,* doubtless
with the intention of boarding, when her superiority in
numbers would have told, and moreover in this
manœuvre lay her last hope of safety, but the *Phœbe*
shook her off, and was about to continue the cannonade, when the French captain hauled down the light at
the masthead and called out that he surrendered.   His
loss, out of 330 men, was 20 killed and 55 wounded,
and that of the *Phœbe* only 13 in all, which thus
conclusively showed the better training of the British

H

seamen. The *Nereide* was purchased into the service and will be heard of again.

The night of Captain Barlow's victory witnessed the capture off Dungeness of the *Growler*, brig of 10 guns and 50 men, by two French privateers, which boarded her by surprise in the dead of night, when, being outnumbered as three to one, the British crew were overpowered, though not until her commander, Lieutenant Hollingsworth, and his second officer were mortally wounded.

During the year the Spanish island of Trinidad was captured by a British naval and military expedition, but an attempt made on Porto Rico met with a repulse and the enterprise was abandoned, with the loss of 225 killed, wounded, and missing. However, about this time the 74's *Thunderer* and *Valiant* destroyed the French 36-gun frigate *Hermione*, which had taken shelter in a port in the island of St. Domingo, and the boats of her English namesake cut out a brig and several smaller vessels from under the batteries in Porto Rico. A singular incident attaches to this 32-gun frigate, which was commanded by Captain Hugh Pigot—an officer of a tyrannical character and much detested by the crew. On the night of the 22nd September they mutinied, and on the first lieutenant coming forward to inquire into the cause of the *émeute* they cut his throat and threw the body overboard. The captain ran on deck, but was driven back into his cabin, where he was set upon and stabbed, and then cast overboard though yet living. In the same barbarous manner eight officers were treated, and those only spared were the master, a midshipman and two warrant officers, the gunner and carpenter. The mutineers then sailed the frigate into La Guayra on the Venezuela coast, and gave her up to the Spanish authorities, who fitted her out with 44 guns, and sent her to sea with a crew of 321 men, exclusive of 72 soldiers. Thus she remained in their hands until October, 1799, when she was cut out by the 28-gun frigate *Surprise*, Captain Edward Hamilton—an exploit of as daring a character as anything recorded even in the history of the British navy, prolific as it is in such deeds. On the evening of the 21st October the *Surprise* arrived off Puerto Cabello, where the *Hermione* was lying moored between two batteries at the entrance of the harbour, and after having carefully reconnoitred her and taken his measures, on the evening of the 24th Captain Hamilton mustered his crew, and informed them of his determination to make the attempt to re-capture the frigate and asked for volunteers, when all hands stepped forward and declared their willingness to follow him.

At eight o'clock that night Captain Hamilton was under way with all the frigate's boats, manned by 100 officers and men, leaving 97 behind, who were

directed to bring the ship off the harbour's mouth.
After a pull of nearly four hours they encountered the
launch of the *Hermione* rowing guard, which, discovering the approach of the boats, retreated and
aroused the crew of the Spanish frigate, who opened
fire with her guns. Pushing on, nothing daunted,
Captain Hamilton about half an hour after midnight
reached the ship, and springing up the side reached
the forecastle, while the gig boarded on the port bow.
Meantime the two cutters boarding on either gangway
amidships had been beaten off, but reinforced by the
launch and jolly-boat, which had been employed in
cutting the bow and stern cables, the British seamen
made good their footing, while the boats proceeded to
tow the frigate out. On her decks, meanwhile, a
desperate struggle went on, but success crowned the
effort from the very hardihood of the attack made by
Captain Hamilton, who quite came up to the standard
laid down by Sir Edward Howard, Lord High Admiral
of the Fleet in Henry VIII.'s reign, that "a naval
officer to be good for anything must be half mad."
While the battle raged fiercely on the quarter-deck,
the rest of the ship forward being in possession of the
Surprise's tars, some men betook themselves aloft and
loosened sail, and when the boats began to pull the
ship from under the batteries as though she were
already won, the Spaniards lost heart and ran below,
where they were closely followed by their persistent

enemy, and the struggle was renewed on the main-
deck until, after a terrible butchery, the survivors
called for quarter. As soon as the prize was seen to
be under way the shore batteries opened fire, and a
24-pound shot passing through her below water; the
pumps were rigged to keep her afloat, and by 2 A.M.
she was out of gunshot. Well was the frigate named
which achieved this surprising capture, and that with
only 12 wounded, including Captain Hamilton
severely in several places, and the gunner dangerously;
and the wonder is increased having regard to the fact
that out of 365 Spaniards on board no less than 119
were killed and 97 wounded. The prize was restored to
the navy under the name of *Retribution*, and Captain
Hamilton was knighted and received the freedom of
the City of London, while the Jamaica House of
Assembly presented him with a sword of the value of
300 guineas. In April of the following year, while
on his passage to England for the better treatment
of his wounds, from which he suffered to the end of
his days, the packet bearing the hero home was
captured by a privateer, and on his arrival at Paris he
was sent for by Buonaparte, who complimented him
on his valour.

CHAPTER IV.

THE year 1798 was signalised above any other event
by Nelson's victory in Aboukir Bay, and among
single ship actions, one, the most noteworthy, was
that between the 74's, *Mars*, Captain Alexander
Hood, and *Hercule*, Captain Heritier, anchored at
the entrance of the Passage du Raz, about twenty-
one miles from Brest, which she was endeavouring
to reach. The *Mars* also brought to ahead of the

enemy, but as the cable ran out she dropped astern,
and the two ships, rubbing sides, commenced to
engage at 9.30 P.M., another night engagement like
so many before particularised. The fighting that
ensued from the propinquity of the ships was of a
most desperate and sanguinary character, for so close
were the muzzles of the contending guns, that those
on the lower deck could not be run out to be discharged, but were fired in-board. The only spar,
therefore, lost in the action was the jibboom of the
Mars, but the danger to the hulls of the combatants
was very great, the starboard side of the *Hercule*
being riddled, and many of the spaces between the
ports laid open, while five of her lower-deck guns
were dismounted, and the contrast between her starboard side, burnt as black as a cinder, and the port,
still of a bright yellow, was most singular.

Exactly within an hour from the commencement
of the action the French 74 struck her colours; but,
sad to say, the gallant Hood did not survive to wear
the laurels he had so nobly won, being hit by a
musket-ball in the femoral artery, and with him
died, out of a crew of 634 all told, Captain White
of the marines, Mr. Midshipman Blythe, and 19
seamen and marines, besides eight missing, probably
killed, and 60 were wounded, including two of the
lieutenants and one midshipman. Of 680 men with
which the *Hercule* began the action, the French

acknowledge to a loss of 290, though the English accounts place it as high as 400. The combatants were evenly matched, as their broadside weight of metal was within one pound the same, while, as is shown, the advantage in strength of crew was on the side of the French 74, though it should be noted that the latter had only been commissioned twenty-four hours, and the *Mars*, as one of the fleet of Lord Bridport (whose nephew her captain was, and also of Lord Hood), had been at sea for a considerable time, and was manned with what Lord St. Vincent called " a well-practised crew." The *Hercule*, which had only been launched ten months, was navigated in safety to Plymouth and added to the navy, and Lieutenant Butterfield, upon whom the command devolved on the death of Captain Hood, received promotion.

During the next few years some gallant exploits were performed in the Channel by British seamen while attacking the flotilla assembled at all the French ports for the invasion of England, and it was not till the crushing defeat of Trafalgar showed the futility of all such attempts that Napoleon dispersed the armament, though it was shortly before that " crowning mercy," as Cromwell called his victory of Dunbar, that the French Emperor broke up his " Grand Army of Invasion," which had so long been encamped at Boulogne, and commenced that march on the Danube which resulted in Austerlitz—an

event that broke the heart of the great William Pitt.
Sir Francis Laforey, commanding the *Hydra*, 38,
after a running flight, compelled the 36-gun frigate
Confiante to run ashore about three leagues from
Havre, and on the following day Captain Laforey
sent his boats to haul down the colours of the
Frenchman and burn her—a service which was suc-
cessfully performed under fire from the beach.

The French now renewed their attempt to invade
Ireland, and on the 6th August, 1798, Commodore
Savary got under weigh from Rochefort with four
frigates, carrying 1,150 soldiers, under the command
of General Humbert, who had accompanied Generals
Hoche and Grouchy in the previous abortive expedition to Bantry Bay. The squadron managed to
avoid the ubiquitous British frigates, and the troops
were landed at Killala Bay, when the French ships
returned in safety to Brest, but General Humbert
was not equally fortunate, and, not receiving the
support he anticipated from the disaffected Irish,
was compelled, after some skirmishes, to surrender
on the 8th September at Ballinamuck to General
Lake.

On the 16th September a second division of the
army for the invasion of Ireland, numbering 3,000
troops, sailed from Brest on board eight frigates, and
the *Hoche*, 74 (so named from the young general
who had died on the 18th September in the pre-

ceding year—a leader of such genius that Buonaparte
was jealous of him), flying the broad pennant of
Commodore Bompart, who commanded the *Embuscade* in the action with the *Boston* early in the war.
On the day after their departure the squadron was
sighted by the 38-gun frigates *Boadicea*, Captain
Goodwin Keats, and *Ethalion*, Captain Countess, and
18-gun brig *Sylph*, Commander White, when Captain
Keats made sail to communicate the news to Lord
Bridport, leaving the others to watch the movements
of the enemy.   Captain Countess was reinforced by
the *Amelia*, 38, Captain the Hon. Charles Herbert,
and *Anson*, 44, Captain Durham, and on learning
their destination despatched the *Sylph* to apprise
the British commander on the Irish coast.   The
three frigates closely dogged the French squadron, but lost sight of them on the 7th October,
though on arriving off the coast of Ireland Commodore Bompart found himself surrounded by Sir
John Warren's squadron, consisting of the 74's,
Canada, *Robust*, and *Foudroyant* (then newly
launched), with the frigates *Magnanime*, *Melampus*,
and *Immortalité*, together with the *Ethalion*, *Anson*,
and *Amelia*.   A close engagement ensued between
the *Hoche* and *Canada*, Captain Thornborough, but
the other ships coming up and taking part in the
action, the French 74, after a gallant resistance, was
compelled to surrender, when reduced to the con-

dition of a wreck, with the loss of 270 out of 1,237 seamen and soldiers on board.

Soon after the *Embuscade* struck her flag to the *Magnanime*, her loss being 15 killed and 26 wounded. The *Loire* and *Immortalité*, the nearest of the seven remaining French frigates, succeeded in crossing the bows of the *Foudroyant* in their attempt to escape, but the *Bellone*, being a bad sailer, could not manage to do so, and having sustained a running fire from several ships, was brought to action by the *Ethalion*, and, after a spirited resistance, hauled down the tri-colour, with the loss of 20 killed and 45 wounded. The *Coquille* also struck, her casualties being 18 and 31 respectively. Of the remaining five frigates, the *Loire* encountered the *Anson*, which had hitherto been too far distant to take part in the engagement, but managing to disable her opponent aloft, the *Loire* made sail to escape, and all of her consorts, in passing to leeward, also exchanged broadsides with Captain Durham's ship. The total loss of the British squadron was 13 killed and 75 wounded, out of which the *Robust* in her action with the *Hoche* had ten killed and her first lieutenant and 39 officers and men wounded, while the total casualty roll of the enemy was no less than 462.

While the other ships were escorting the prizes, the *Canada, Foudroyant*, and *Melampus* gave chase to the five retreating frigates, and the last overtook the *Résolue*, 36, which, after a feeble resistance, surrendered, though this was in no way due, it is only right to say, to want of gallantry on the part of Captain Bargeau, but his ship was old, and her main-deck ports were closed to keep out the heavy sea that was running.

Of the remaining four frigates, the *Loire* and *Immortalité* were destined to fare no better than their consorts. The former and the *Sémillante* were sighted by the *Revolutionaire*, 38, Captain Twysden, *Mermaid*, 32, Captain Newman, and *Kangaroo*, 18-gun brig, Commander Brace, and they parted company, when the *Revolutionaire* chased one and the *Mermaid* the *Loire*, with which the *Kangaroo* was first to engage in the most gallant manner, until her fore-topmast was shot away, when she dropped astern. Early the following morning the *Mermaid*, a frigate of little more than half her broadside weight of metal, with over 100 fewer men, closely engaged the enemy, but though she shot away the *Loire's* fore-topmast and inflicted other damage, she herself lost her mizen-mast by the board, and also the main-topmast, and was almost reduced to the condition of a wreck aloft, her rigging, standing and running, and boats being cut to pieces, while her hull was penetrated by many shot, causing her to make much water, and as a gale of wind came on, in which her foremast was carried away, the ship with the utmost difficulty was brought into Lough Swilly. The *Loire*, instead of boarding her helpless opponent, when her crew of 624 soldiers and sailors must have triumphed over 208 British seamen, made sail, but only to encounter a more formidable adversary in the *Anson*, 44, which had lost her mizen-mast, the *Loire* being without her fore and main-topmasts. The action began about 10.30 on the following day, and on the brig *Kangaroo* arriving on the scene, the French frigate, whose mizen-mast went over the side, hailed to say she had surrendered. The loss on this occasion was admitted by a French account to be 46 killed and 71 wounded, but what her loss had been in her previous action with the *Mermaid* was not stated.

We have already detailed the capture of the *Immortalité*, another of Commodore Bompart's ships by the *Fisgard*, and the whole of the seven prizes were brought to Plymouth, the *Hoche* being re-named the *Donegal* (under which designation she was engaged in Duckworth's victory at St. Domingo), the *Embuscade* the *Seine*, which, together with the *Loire* and *Revolutionaire*, performed excellent service under their new flag, but the *Coquille* caught fire and blew up at Hamoaze, and the *Bellone* and *Résolue* were found to be too worn out for further service afloat. The uncaptured frigates of Bompart's squadron, *Romaine* and *Sémillante*, arrived in safety at Brest and Lorient. Promotion to the rank of commander was given to the first lieutenants of the *Canada*, flagship, *Robust* (to which the capture of the *Hoche* was chiefly due), *Fisgard*, which took the *Immortalité* unaided, and *Ethalion*, the conqueror of the *Bellone*, to whose captain it was chiefly due that Commodore Bompart's squadron was dogged so unceasingly to the coast of Ireland.

On the very day the *Hoche* was captured the fourth expedition, despatched for the same destination, came to an abortive termination. The first was scattered by storms in December, 1796, the second, under Commodore Savary, disembarked troops in August, 1798, but only for them to surrender in the following month ; the failure of the third we have just detailed, and the last was that of Savary, who again sailed from Rochefort with four frigates, having some troops on board ; but on his arrival at Killala Bay he learned the disastrous fate that had befallen General Humbert's army and Commodore Bompart's fleet, and, steering for France, narrowly escaped capture from a British squadron, and re-entered Rochefort three weeks after sailing thence.

As a result of the naval operations of the four years since the war began there were no less than 30,000 prisoners of war confined in British prisons, while our loss in captured seamen and marines during the same period was only 2,800—numbers which afford a fair comparison of the relative success of the French and English fleets.

A very brilliant defence was made by the armed tender *George*, of six guns and 40 men, Lieutenant Mackey, against two Spanish privateers, and it was not till she had lost more than half of her crew, which numbered less than three-fourths the number of the enemy, that the *George* surrendered. On the other hand, the *Cheri*, 26, struck to the 40-gun frigate *Pomone*, having lost in the gallant attempt to drive off a superior enemy, 15 killed, including her commander, and 19 wounded ; but the *Cheri* was so much damaged that she sank alongside. A more equal encounter was that between the *Kingfisher*, 18, Captain Pierrepoint, and the French privateer *Betsey*, which surrendered after a spirited defence ; but the odds were greatly on the French side, when Lieutenant Pym of the British 20-gun ship *Babet*, with the pinnace and launch, having 24 men, of which only the pinnace was engaged, boarded and cut out the *Desirée*, of six guns and 46 men, of whom three were killed, eight drowned, and 15 wounded, Lieutenant Pym and Mr. Midshipman Aslinhurst being wounded with six out of her dozen hands, besides two who perished.

The 36-gun frigate *Melampus*, Captain Moore, captured the *Volage*, of 22 guns and 195 men, after a brief action, and the *Speedy*, 14 (which afterwards earned such glory under Lord Cochrane) closely engaged the privateer *Papillon*, of like force, which managed, however, to make good her escape, but she re-took a prize that had fallen into the hands of the fugitive. The cutter *Marquis Cobourg*, of 12 guns and 66 men, also engaged after a chase of 100 miles the privateer *Revanche*, of 16 guns and 62 men, which, after a spirited resistance, struck her colours, but she was so much damaged by more than 40 shot between wind and water that she sank, nearly taking with her all on board. Another privateer of the same name, carrying 10 guns and 54 men, also surrendered to the 10-gun schooner *Recovery*, Lieutenant Ross, after an action lasting three-quarters of an hour, which was a very creditable performance, as the British crew of between 40 and 50 hands were described by the *Recovery's* commander as being chiefly young and inexperienced lads, who behaved with the valour and coolness of veteran seamen.

The 14-gun brig *Victorieuse*, Captain Dickson, chased two French privateers off Guadaloupe, and compelled one of them, the *Brutus*, of 12 guns and 80 men, to strike after a brief resistance. This was on the 7th May, and on the 3rd December, in company with the *Zephyr*, 14, Captain Champion, she attacked two forts in the island of Margarita, a Spanish possession, and though garrisoned by 300

men, carried them both and bore off a French privateer of six guns and 80 men that had run there for
protection.

Of frigate actions we have to record one off the
island of Sicily between the *Seahorse*, Captain Foote,
and the *Sensible*, having 36 guns and 300 men, but
the superiority of force was decidedly on the side
of the British frigate, which, though nominally a 38,
carried 46 guns. The *Sensible* surrendered after a
running fight and a short close action, when she had
lost 18 killed and 37 wounded, and her rigging and
spars were much cut up, while she received 36 shot
between wind and water. The British frigates *Sibylle*,
Captain Edward Cooke, and *Fox*, Captain Pulteney
Malcolm, being disguised, entered the Spanish port
of Manilla, the capital of the Philippines, and passing
as two of Admiral Sercey's French squadrons, were
boarded by the Spanish Admiral and others, whom
Captains Cooke and Malcolm detained, and captured
three gun-boats without firing a shot, and when the
captain of the port came off in a felucca to inquire
into these strange proceedings, he also was made
prisoner. Further concealment being now impossible,
the frigates, in the presence of the seventy-fours
Europa, Magnanime, and *San Pedro Apostol,* made
sail with the three gun-boats, one of which foundered
in a heavy squall of wind, carrying with her the prize
crew. The *Sibylle* and *Fox* suffered a repulse from

I

some forts at Magindanao, where they purposed to lay
in a supply of wood and water, and at another
harbour on the same island the boat's crews, while
watering, were attacked by the natives, when three
were killed and nine carried into the interior, though
they were eventually restored.

In January the frigates *Vertu*, Commodore Magon,
and *Régénérée*, Captain Willaumez, sailed from Mauritius for France with letters from Tippo Sahib, who was
desirous of concluding a treaty with the French Re-
public with the object of driving the English out of
India, and who, relying on the aid of the troops at
Mauritius, commenced the war which ended in his
defeat and death at Seringapatam in the following
year. Off the west coast of Africa these frigates
engaged the *Pearl*, 32, Captain Ballard, which shook
them off and arrived safely at Sierra Leone. Continuing their course for France, they sighted off the
port of Santa Cruz the 28-gun frigate *Brilliant*,
Captain Henry Blackwood (Nelson's friend and captain of the *Euryalus*, in which he joined the fleet off
Cadiz just before Trafalgar), which kept up a running
fight all day, when, finding the enemy overhauling
him, Captain Blackwood bore up athwart the bows of
the *Régénérée* and gave her a broadside, shooting
away her main-topmast, when the French frigate
dropped astern. Having repaired damages she renewed the chase, but the *Brilliant* maintained her

fire on both frigates as they approached with her stern-chasers, and during the night out-distanced her pursuers, the *Régénérée* having lost her bowsprit, foremast, and main-topmast.

The 36-gun frigate *Preneuse*, another of Admiral Sercey's squadron, after capturing two Indiamen at Tellicherry, which made some resistance, steered for Batavia, and in the following year (1799) made her way to South Africa, and at Algoa Bay found the sloop-of-war *Rattlesnake*, 16, and armed store-ship *Camel*, which she engaged on the evening of the 20th September. The commanders being both on shore, Lieutenants Fothergill and Shaw opened fire at 8.30 P.M., and continued the action till 3.30 on the following morning, when the *Preneuse*, slipping her cable, made sail, leaving the honours of war to her opponents, whose gallant defence against superior force was very creditable to the young officers. On hearing what had happened the *Jupiter*, 50, Captain Granger, sailed from Table Bay in quest of the *Preneuse*, and sighted her on the 10th October, when a running fight ensued during the whole of that night; but the *Jupiter*, which, owing to the heavy sea, had to keep her lower-deck ports closed, bore away to repair damages, and the French frigate escaped. Her career, however, was short, for on her return to Mauritius she was sighted by the *Tremendous*, 74, Captain Osborn, and *Adamant*, 50, Captain Hotham, and finding escape impossible, Captain l'Hermite ran his ship ashore, where, though lying under the fire of some batteries, she was boarded by the boats of the British ships, under Lieutenant Grey, and set on fire and destroyed in the most gallant manner.

Another of Admiral Sercey's squadron, the *Seine*, 40, commanded by Lieutenant Bigot, met with an equally disastrous termination to her cruise, and that within sight of the shores of France, whither she had sailed. After a favourable voyage she was close to Brest, when the frigates *Jason*, 36, Captain Stirling, *Pique*, 36, Captain Milne, and *Mermaid*, 32, Captain Newman, appeared in sight and barred the entrance to the port. A running fight ensued between the *Seine* and *Pique*, which losing her main-topmast, dropped astern, when the *Jason* came up; but all three soon after grounded, the *Jason* being exposed to a heavy raking fire, but seeing the approach of the *Mermaid*, Lieutenant Bigot, who had made a gallant defence, hauled down his colours. The loss of the *Seine*, out of 610 men, was 170 killed and 100 wounded, that of the two British frigates engaged being only nine killed and 18 wounded. Every attempt having failed to float the *Pique*, to which her capture was chiefly due, she was destroyed, but the *Jason* and *Seine* were got afloat, and Captain Milne and his crew were turned over to the prize, which he commissioned under her own name.

A melancholy loss befell our squadron in the East Indies in the destruction by blowing up of the *Resistance*, 44, Captain Pakenham, when 332 souls perished. The survivors, 13 seamen, constructed a raft on which seven reached the coast of Sumatra, but only one of them, Scott, a quartermaster, was released by the Malays into whose hands they fell, and the other eight who remained on the raft were never heard of again. It was one of the most terrible and complete disasters that even the annals of the sea can show.

Nearer home the *Flora*, 36, Captain Middleton, chased the corvette *Mondovi*, 18, into Cerigo, in the Greek Archipelago, when her boats, commanded by Lieutenant Russell, cut the enemy out in the most gallant manner, under a heavy fire from the forts. The *Regulus*, while cruising off the island of Porto Rico, discovered some vessels lying at anchor in Aguada Bay, when Captain Eyre sent his boats, under command of Lieutenant Good, to cut them out, and that brave officer succeeded in bringing out three of the largest of them, though they lay under the protection of a battery. Still more remarkable was the feat of arms achieved by Lieutenant Shortland, of the 38-gun frigate *Melpomene*, whose boats, and those of the brig *Childers*, carrying 70 officers and men under his command, at 10 o'clock on the night of the 3rd August, entered a port on the Isle Bas, on the coast of France, after a pull of five hours, and, though

they encountered a stubborn resistance, carried off
the 14-gun brig *Aventurier*, which lost 16 out of her
crew of 79 hands. Shortland was promoted for his
gallantry on this occasion.

During the night of the 5th July a desperate action
took place between the corvette *Lodi*, of 18 guns and
130 men, which was carrying despatches from Leghorn to Alexandria for Buonaparte, and the British
privateer *Eagle*, carrying 14 guns and 57 men.
Twice the British privateer's crew, severely galled by
the enemy's musketry, attempted to board, but were
driven back by superior numbers, when the French
made a similar attempt, but with a like want of success, and about 3 A.M. the *Eagle*, with only the
stump of her mainmast standing, got away, the *Lodi*
making no endeavour to arrest her flight.

Captain Dixon, of the 64-gun ship *Lion*, sighted
off Carthagena, on the Spanish coast, four 34-gun
frigates, and shortening sail bore down upon them as
they lay in line of battle awaiting his attack. Cutting
off the *Santa Dorotea*, he brought her to close action,
and notwithstanding some feeble attempts of the
others to succour their consort, compelled her to
haul down her colours with a loss of 20 killed and
32 wounded out of 371, which showed that the
Spanish captain had done all that the most puncti-
lious demands of honour could require, though his
brother commanders failed to give him the support

he might have anticipated.   The prize was added to
the navy under her own name.

A spirited fight took place between the 14-gun
brig *Espoir*, Captain Otway Bland, and the Genoese
pirate *Liguria* (as James calls her), of 26 guns and
120 men.   The captain of the *Liguria* with considerable assurance hailed the little man-of-war to
strike or he would sink her, enforcing his threat
with a broadside, but got a reply that took him
aback in a shower of cannon-balls.   The vessels became
closely engaged, when the Genoese commander hailed,
begging Captain Bland to cease firing.   The British
officer ordered him to come on board, but as instead
of doing so he shot ahead as though with the intention of raking the *Espoir*, Captain Bland resumed his
fire, and about 11 P.M. the enemy lowered her sails
and ceased firing.   Commander Bland was posted
for his gallantry on this occasion, and his subsequent
career proved him to be an enterprising officer.   Sir
Edward Pellew, of the *Indefatigable*, captured after
a twenty-four hours' chase the French corvette *Vail-
lante*, of 20 guns and 175 men, which was added
to the service under the name of *Danae*.   A few
days later the *Hazard*, 18, Captain Butterfield,
engaged the French armed ship *Neptune*, having on
board 320 seamen and soldiers, who made an attempt
to board the British ship-of-war, but were repulsed,
when the *Neptune* surrendered.

But the most sanguinary and not the least glorious achievement of British seamen during the year 1798, though it resulted in defeat, was the defence of the 50-gun frigate *Leander*, against the *Généreux*, 74. This ship, with the *Guillaume Tell*, was the only one that escaped out of the French fleet Nelson defeated on the 1st of August in Aboukir Bay, five days after which the *Leander* sailed from Alexandria with his despatches. At daybreak on the 18th Captain Boulden Thompson, her commander, sighted the 74, and not feeling justified in engaging, if it could be avoided, so superior an antagonist, made sail, but finding that the stranger gained upon him, he shortened sail and awaited his gigantic enemy. The action began soon after 9 A.M., and after an hour and a half's cannonading the *Généreux* ran the *Leander* on board, which was so cut up aloft as to be unmanageable. The French, who mustered 936 to 282, determined to put their superiority to account, and made many attempts to board, but each time they were repulsed by the marines on the poop and small-arm men on the quarter-deck, while the ships, as they lay with their sides grinding against each other, continued the discharge of cannon. It forms a splendid tribute to the valour of the *Leander's* crew that, with an inferiority that rendered success hopeless, they continued the conflict and there was no talk of surrender, in which there could be no disgrace, while

HERBERT BROWN

"THE BRITISH FRIGATE POURED INTO THE FRENCHMAN EVERY GUN FROM HER STARBOARD BROADSIDE."

it would save a useless effusion of blood. The *Généreux*, clearing herself of the British frigate, forged ahead, but the latter, whose mizen-mast was hanging over the starboard quarter, her foremast over the port bow, and her lower yards on the booms, managed to bear up and poured into the Frenchman every gun from her starboard broadside. The action was fought almost in a dead calm, with the sea like a mill-pond, and the *Généreux*, which had only lost her mizen-topmast, having now taken up a position across the *Leander's* stern, which would have enabled her to rake her at will, Captain Thompson, in reply to the hail of the French commander, replied that he surrendered his ship, which (there being no boat available, all having been destroyed) was taken possession of by the boatswain and a midshipman, who swam on board.

In this six hours' close and sanguinary conflict the *Leander*, out of a crew numbering less than 300, had three midshipmen and 32 seamen and marines killed, and 57 wounded, among whom were Captain Thompson (severely in three places) Captain Berry, Nelson's flag-captain at the Nile, two lieutenants, the master, boatswain, one master's mate, and a midshipman. This was one-third of her crew, of whom 14 had been wounded at Aboukir Bay, while the *Généreux*, which commenced the action with 936 hands, had 100 killed, including her first lieutenant, and 188 wounded — a number actually equalling the entire crew of her prize ! In weight of metal the disparity was no less great, for with 80 guns to the *Leander's* 51 the respective broadsides were 1,024 and 432 pounds. When Captains Thompson and Berry reached England on their release from Corfu, whither the *Leander* was carried, he and his officers and men were tried by court-martial, whose verdict was that " The gallant and almost unprecedented defence of Captain Thompson of H.M.'s late ship *Leander* against so superior a force as that of the *Généreux* is deserving of every praise his country and this court can give, and that his conduct, as well as that of his officers and men under his command, reflects not only the highest honour on himself and them, but on their country at large." Captain Thompson on his return to the shore from the *Stately,* on board of which the court-martial was held at Sheerness, was cheered by all the ships in harbour, and both he and Captain Berry were knighted.

It is satisfactory to add that the *Généreux* was captured eighteen months later by Lord Nelson, whose flag was then in the *Foudroyant,* while in company with the *Alexander,* Captain Ball, and *Success,* frigate, when Admiral Perrée was killed, and her fate, in which was involved that of 2,000 soldiers she had on board, sealed that of Malta, which soon after surrendered. But this event did not take place until the *Guillaume Tell,* the last ship of the French Nile fleet, surrendered after a gallant resistance to a squadron consisting of the *Foudroyant*, Sir Edward Berry, *Lion*, 64, Captain Dixon, and 36-gun frigate *Penelope*, Captain the Hon. Henry Blackwood, which had first sighted the 74, and hung on to and engaged her till the others came up.

The French 36-gun frigate *Decade*, Captain Villeneuve, surrendered to the British frigates *Naiad* and *Magnanime*, after a running fight, and the *Flora* struck to the *Anson* and *Phaeton*—a ship which, launched in 1757, had been captured four years later by the 28-gun frigate *Unicorn*, and being added to the British navy was sunk by her crew at Rhode Island in 1778, to prevent her falling into the hands of the Americans, who weighed the frigate, and then sold her to the French Government. The 36-gun frigate *Sirius*, Captain King, captured the *Furie*, a Dutch ship-of-war of much inferior force, after a running action, and she was added to the service under the name of *Wilhelmina*. Mention should be made of the gallantry of the crew of the British privateer *Herald*, Captain Pistock, who beat off, near Naples, three French privateers, leaving them in a shattered condition with the loss of 30 men. Captain Fahie, of the 22-gun ship *Perdrix*, also captured a French 18-gun privateer, after a sixteen hours' chase and a sharp action of three-quarters of an hour's duration.

On the other side of the account must be placed the action between the 32-gun frigate *Ambuscade*, Captain Jenkins, and the 28-gun frigate *Baionnaise*, which resulted in the loss of the former after a desperate action. The victory was gained by the boarders of the French ship, and the respective numbers were 190 and 250; but, nevertheless, it was discreditable to the British crew, who had been disheartened by the bursting of a gun on the maindeck, when 11 were wounded and that part of the ship wrecked, and later by an explosion which blew out a part of the stern and placed *hors de combat* all the gun's crew. Before her surrender with the loss of 10 killed and 36 wounded the first lieutenant and master had been slain, the captain, the only other lieutenant, and the marine officer were wounded, and the command devolved upon the purser, which so discouraged the crew, who were also apprehensive of the magazine blowing up, that they abandoned their quarters. That a little perseverance might have changed the aspect of affairs may be gathered from the fact that the French loss exceeded theirs, being 30 killed and 30 severely wounded, including the captain, first lieutenant, and officer in command of the troops. The prize was re-named the *Embuscade*, a word of pleasant memory to the French marine, as one of the name had the best of the encounter with the *Boston*. The *Baionnaise* at a subsequent period was driven on shore and destroyed by the *Ardent*. This unfortunate affair concluded the single-ship actions in 1798.

As that year was chiefly famous as regards these encounters for that between the *Leander* and *Généreux*, so 1799 was remarkable for the action between the French frigate *Forte* and the *Sibylle*, Captain Edward Cooke, the same who with the *Fox* had so boldly entered Manilla and carried off three gun-boats under the eyes of three Spanish ships-of-the-line. The *Forte*, a fine frigate carrying 52 guns and 370 men, was commanded by Captain Beaulieu-le-Long, one of the most enterprising of those officers who had been harrying with great success British commerce in the Indian seas, and on the 19th February Captain Cooke sailed from Madras in quest of her. The ships were not ill matched, as the *Sibylle*, formerly a 40-gun frigate captured by the *Romney*, 60, in June, 1794, though one-third less in tonnage, carried 48 guns, throwing a broadside weight of metal of 503 pounds, to 604, that of the *Forte's*, with a crew about the same as that of her antagonist, which had sent away 143 officers and men in the prizes she had made in the Bay of Bengal. The meeting so much desired, which had so glorious a result for British arms and for the gallant Cooke, who fell at the moment of victory, came about in a dramatic manner. It was by the flashes of her guns on a dark night, as the *Forte* was taking possession of two rich prizes bound for China, that the French frigate betrayed her presence, and steering towards her, shortly before midnight on the 28th February, Captain Cooke saw the lights of three ships lying-to, and judging from the brilliant display of one of the number, whose two rows of ports were all lit up, that she was the long-sought-for enemy, he steered towards her, and soon found his anticipations verified, as she opened fire, bringing down the *Sibylle's* jib. Reserving her fire, she steered steadily on, just as the *Victory* did at Trafalgar when nearing the enemy's line, and when arrived at less than pistol-shot range, at three-quarters past midnight, Captain Cooke, putting his helm up, raked the *Forte* fore and aft with deadly effect, and, luffing up, poured a second broadside into her as she ranged up alongside. The battle now raged furiously, but the crew of the French frigate, apparently disconcerted by those two tremendous broadsides, never recovered their coolness, and delivered too elevated a fire, which rattled harmlessly through the shrouds, whilst almost every shot of the *Sibylle's* found its billet in the hull and crowded decks of the Frenchman. At 1.30 Captain Cooke was mortally wounded by a grape-shot, and delegated the command to Lieutenant Hardyman; and soon after Captain Davies, a military officer on board, *aide-de-camp* to Lord Mornington, the Governor-General, while encouraging the men at the quarter-deck guns, was killed by a cannon-shot. Three-quarters of an hour later the *Forte* ceased firing, and was hailed to know if she surrendered, but no answer being returned the cannonade was resumed. A second time the enemy were hailed, but there was no response, and the British continued to work the guns with such vigour that her mizen-mast went over the side, and was followed a few minutes later by the other masts and bowsprit, when all chance of escape being over and the ship lying a helpless hulk, the gallant tars of the *Sibylle* hailed their success with three cheers and all firing ceased, within about two and a half hours from the commencement of the engagement.

The *Sibylle* now dropped her anchor in 17 fathoms of water, the action having taken place off the Sandheads at the entrance to the Hooghly, and the crew set to work repairing damages, which were very considerable aloft, all the *Sibylle's* running rigging and sails being cut to pieces and masts and yards badly wounded. But her loss was only five killed and 17 wounded, while that of the *Forte* was almost unprecedented, and the sight that met the eye of the third lieutenant of the *Sibylle*, who went on board the prize to take possession, was such as to beggar description. Not only were all the boats shot away, but she had not a spar left standing, and the masts lay in the sea alongside with all the sails set, while

the bowsprit was cut away close to the figure-head ;
also the *Forte's* starboard side was nearly all beaten
in from stem to stern, and upwards of 300 shot were
counted in her hull, while several of her guns were
dismounted, and the decks were ploughed up with
missiles. Out of 370 men she had lost 65 killed,
including her captain and first lieutenant, and 80
wounded, among whom were many officers.   On the
prize being rigged with jury-masts the ships sailed
for Calcutta, when Lieutenant (then Commander)
Hardyman commissioned the *Forte*, which, however,
was soon lost in the Red Sea.

In the ill-fated military expedition to Holland the
navy had but little part, but a detachment of 157
seamen and marines, under Captain Boorder, distinguished itself by the defence of Lemmers-town, in
West Friesland, when they beat off a body of 700
French and Dutch troops, who lost 25 killed and 29
wounded.   During the expedition, the naval portion
of which was under the command of Admiral Mitchell,
three ships were wrecked, the *Nassau*, 64, and
Blanche and *Lutine* frigates, the latter of which had
£140,000 on board.   Memorable also was the loss
of the 28-gun frigate *Proserpine*, Captain Wallis, on
the sands off Cuxhaven at the mouth of the Elbe.
The crew had to abandon their ships on the 1st
February, and after suffering incredible hardships,
when twelve men were frozen to death while making

their way for six miles over the ice, the officers and men reached the town of Cuxhaven.

A desperate conflict took place between the *Wolverine*, of 12 guns and 70 men, and two French luggers, carrying 150 hands, who, taking advantage of their superior numbers, ran alongside, one on either hand, and tried to carry the brig by boarding. Captain Mortlock headed his men, with his own hand running one daring fellow through the body with his pike, and the privateers were beaten off with heavy loss, both their commanders being among the killed, and the gallant Mortlock shared their fate, after receiving wounds in the head, breast, and loins, though he refused to leave the deck, his last words being as he fell " Luff, luff, keep close to them ! " Such were the officers who led their crews to victory, and heroes of the type of Cooke and Mortlock formed the generality of the commanders of our ships.

Of Admiral Sercey's squadron of frigates cruising in Indian seas we have seen that one of the three which sailed for Europe, the *Seine*, was captured on the coast of France, and the *Vertu* and *Régénérée* reached port in safety after engaging the *Pearl*. Of the three remaining at the commencement of the year the *Forte* and *Preneuse* have also been accounted for, and there was only left the *Prudente*, and when her fate is considered it will appear that the French Indian Squadron was scarcely more fortunate than

K

Commodore Bompart's for the invasion of Ireland, or Admiral Brueys' fleet in Egypt, of which two only escaped from Nelson's clutches at Aboukir Bay, to be captured later on, as already detailed.   Such was the power and so ubiquitous were the British frigates that one of the most surprising incidents of the war was that Napoleon succeeded in crossing the Mediterranean with his great armada for the invasion of Egypt and conquest of Malta without discovery, and also made good his escape to France from Alexandria in a frigate, which eluded the swarm of ships cruising about in the Mediterranean.   But so it was ordered by fate or a Higher Power, and when his unparalleled career of victory and slaughter was brought to a close at Waterloo, he found the escape he sought to America barred by the sleepless vigilance of our frigate captains.

On the 9th February, 1799, less than three weeks before the capture of the *Sibylle*, the *Prudente*, the last of Sercey's squadron—though James speaks of the *Cybele*, which, he says, arrived at Mauritius before the war commenced, and left for France a year or two before these occurrences—was sighted by the *Dœdalus*, Captain Ball, and with her was a prize, on which she had placed, besides a party of 17 men, all but two of her quarter-deck six-pounders.   Her armament thus at the time of the action was 30 guns, and that of the *Dœdalus* 38, so that the British

frigate had the superiority in weight of metal, but
the latter was considerably smaller in size and her
crew numbered 212 to 301 on board the Frenchman.
The enemy's ships separated, when Captain Ball gave
chase to the *Prudente*, which soon after noon
shortened sail and fired a broadside at the *Dædalus*,
which a quarter of an hour later, having also taken
in her top-gallant sails, bore up across the stern of
the *Prudente*, and pouring in a broadside at half
pistol-shot range, luffed up under her lee, when a
brisk engagement ensued, the ships running alongside each other.   As usual the gunnery on either
side was unequal, for while the damage received by
the *Dædalus* was of a trifling character, she inflicted
serious loss on her foe, whose mizen-mast was shot
away within a quarter of an hour, and in an hour
the *Prudente* struck, considerably shattered in hull,
and with a loss of 27 killed and 22 wounded, while
the British frigate had only 14 casualties, two of
which were fatal.

In the Mediterranean the *Argo*, 44, Captain
Bowen, overhauled the Spanish 34-gun frigate *Santa
Teresa*, which after receiving a broadside surrendered,
though as the *Leviathan*, 74, was coming up astern,
resistance would have been useless.   The prize, a
fine new ship only just out of dock, was an acquisition to the British navy.   The *Espoir*, of 14 guns
and 80 men, whose capture by the *Liguria* when

under the command of Captain Sanders we have
described, engaged the Spanish " xebec " frigate
Africa, of like force but with 38 soldiers in addition to her crew, and after the firing had lasted an
hour and a half, Commander Sanders, running alongside the enemy, boarded and captured her after a
sharp struggle in which the Spanish loss was nine
killed and 23 wounded, including the commander,
who informed Captain Sanders while lying wounded
in his cabin, that he fully expected to take the *Espoir*
into Malaga.

Lieutenant Worth, of the armed brig *Telegraph,* of
16 guns and 60 men, achieved a brilliant success,
for which he was promoted, in the capture of the
privateer *Hirondelle,* of like force as to guns but
having 12 more men. The action was fought yard-
arm to yard-arm, each of the crews being equally confident of its ability to carry the other's ship, and
in succession they boarded and were repulsed. For
long the victory hung in the balance, but at length,
after a struggle lasting three hours and a half, the
Hirondelle hauled down her flag, with a loss of 19
killed and wounded. In the West Indies the boats
of the *Trent,* under Lieutenants Belchier and Bal-
derston, covered by the fire of the 12-gun cutter
Sparrow, landed a detachment on Porto Rico, which
stormed a Spanish battery and brought off a ship
and three schooners lying under its protection. Even

more dashing and bold was the success achieved by
the boats of the frigate *Success*, carrying 42 men,
under the command of Lieutenant Facey. Though
the enemy's vessel, bound from Genoa to Barcelona,
mounted 10 guns and had on board 113 hands, and
was supported by a battery, Lieutenant Facey, whose
instructions empowered him to retire if the force
opposed to him appeared too strong, resolved to
make the attempt to cut her out, and with odds
against him of three to one, made a dash for the
Bella Aurora, himself being the first to land on her
deck, and carried her off in triumph, though with the
loss of four killed and Lieutenant Stupart, his
second in command, and eight men badly wounded.
For this brilliant feat of arms Lieutenant Facey was
promoted to the rank of commander.

This contempt for the enemy, whether French or
Spanish, which Nelson carried to the extent of
expressing his belief that a British seaman was worth
any day three of either nationality, was displayed off
Belle Isle, when the *San Fiorenzo*, Sir Harry Neale,
and *Amelia*, Captain the Hon. Charles Herbert
(originally the French frigates *Proserpine* and
Minerve), having approached so near off Lorient that
they were seen by three frigates and a gun-vessel
lying in the roadstead, these weighed anchor in
pursuit. The British frigates, nothing daunted,
awaited the squadron, consisting of the *Cornélie*

Vengeance, and *Sémillante*, though the British were much handicapped, as a squall of wind just then carried away the *Amelia's* main-topmast and fore and mizen-top-gallant masts. Soon after 10 A.M. the French squadron opened fire, to which the British frigates replied; but the enemy seemed disinclined to close, though in such superior force, and three times Captains Neale and Herbert had to bear up in order to be within gunshot. At length, after the action had lasted two hours and a half, the enemy made sail, having suffered heavily, as was afterwards discovered, the loss of the *Cornélie* being, it was said, 100 killed and wounded, including the commodore himself, while the French account in the official *Moniteur* acknowledged that the captain of the *Vengeance* was mortally wounded and the *Sémillante* had 15 killed. The *Amelia* and *San Fiorenzo* had 38 casualties, and were much cut up aloft; and it was incomprehensible that three frigates, in sight of their own port, should in so pusillanimous a manner abandon a conflict with an inferior force.

But French seamen were not incapable of making an heroic defence against heavy odds, as was proved by the action between the *Amaranthe*, Commander Vesey, of 14 guns and 86 men, and the privateer schooner *Vengeur* (worthy to bear the name of the seventy-four that maintained so gallant a fight with the *Brunswick* in Lord Howe's victory), which only carried six small cannon, and had a crew of 36, including passengers. Notwithstanding the great disparity of force the *Vengeur* only struck her flag when 14 men had died and five others were wounded in her defence. Almost equally creditable was the resistance made by the British brig *Fortune* (a prize nine months before to the *Swiftsure*, 74) of 10 guns and 28 men, against the *Salamine*, mounting 16 guns of double the calibre, and with a crew of 126. The conflict took place off Jaffa, on the Syrian coast, where Sir Sidney Smith had sent Lieutenant Davis to cruise in the *Fortune*, with the object of cutting off supplies for the French army then laying siege to Acre, under the command of Buonaparte. The *Fortune* only struck when she had expended all her cartridges, and had six killed and wounded, including her commander.

The British 32-gun frigate *Alcmène*, Captain Digby, brought to close action, after a long chase and running fight, the privateer *Courageux*, of Bordeaux, carrying 28 guns and 253 men, and soon after, learning that some Spanish vessels were in the port of Vivero, on the north-west coast of the peninsula, Captain Digby sent his boats under the command of Lieutenants Warren and Oliver, who brought out two ships under the fire of some forts, to which the *Alcmène*, standing close in, replied with her guns.

Equally meritorious was the conduct of Commander Jahleel Brenton, of the *Speedy*, brig, of 14 guns and 80 men, immortalised by Lord Cochrane a year or two later, when he assumed command of her. In company with the brig *Defender*, Brenton determined to engage three Spanish armed vessels, which had taken shelter in a small sandy bay, and, running in, the *Speedy* anchored within pistol shot and cannonaded them, when the enemy landed, on which the *Speedy's* men boarded them under musketry fire from the shore, and brought them out. Soon after this exploit Captain Brenton pursued some coasters that ran for protection under the guns of a fort near Cape Trafalgar ; but though he silenced the battery he found it impossible, owing to the heavy surf, either to carry off or destroy the vessels. A month later the little *Speedy* was attacked by twelve Spanish gunboats, which came out of Algesiras, but she beat them all off, though she herself suffered severely in hull and rigging.

That enterprising officer, Lieutenant Searle, commanding the 10-gun cutter *Courier*, forming part of a squadron under the command of Captain Sotheron, of the *Latona*, engaged the late British brig *Crash*, of equal force, which, however, held out till the *Pylades* and *Espiègle*, coming on the scene, opened fire on her, and then only surrendered after a very gallant resistance. Lieutenant Searle captured, after a warm engagement, the privateer *Guerrier*, of slightly superior force, which lost 10 men, and the gallant officer at length received the promotion to which his previous services had well entitled him. The boats of Captain Sotheron's squadron made an attempt to cut out the Dutch six-gun schooner *Vengeance*, lying under protection of a battery, the guns of which were spiked; but the schooner, which her crew had abandoned, blew up, fortunately, before the British seamen had established a footing on board.

The British 38-gun frigate *Clyde*, Captain Cunningham, sighted off the port of Rochefort two strange sail, and, giving chase, overhauled the larger, which proved the *Vestale*, 36, the same ship the *Terpsichore* had formerly engaged. An action ensued, which lasted for nearly two hours, when the Frenchman, having been severely handled by her opponent, hauled down the Tricolour, with the loss, out of 230 men, of 10 killed and 22 wounded, the *Clyde* having only five casualties. The shattered condition of the hull and rigging of the *Vestale* proved the accuracy of her adversary's fire; but, nevertheless, that Captain Gaspard did his duty against a ship of superior force, the British commander, with the generosity of an honourable opponent, was not behindhand to testify. His consort *Sagesse*, 28, which left the *Vestale* to her fate on this occasion,

was subsequently captured.   Early in the war it
had been the custom to knight the captains who
had taken French frigates, even when of inferior
force, as in the case of the *Crescent* and *Réunion*,
and *Unité* and *Révolutionaire ;* but this honour was
only conferred at a later period when the captured
vessel was of equal or superior strength, and, therefore, Captain Cunningham received no title, but his
first lieutenant, Mr. Kerr, who had lost an eye in
the action between the *Boston* and *Embuscade*, was
promoted to commander.

A sister ship of the *Clyde*, the *Tamar*, of 46 guns
and 281 men, commanded by Captain Western,
sighted off the island of Surinam (which was taken
from the Dutch about this time) the 32-gun frigate
Républicaine, which, after a long chase, shook off
her pursuer.   On the following morning, however,
the *Tamar* again descried the *Républicaine* and gave
chase, which lasted all day, but at 5.30 in the
evening Captain Western got alongside the enemy
and brought her to action.   With such odds against
her the French frigate could not hope to make a
successful resistance, though had the nationality of
the combatants been changed more than ten minutes
would have been necessary to reduce her opponent
to submission.   The *Républicaine*, however, at the
end of that short space of time was brought to the
condition of a wreck, with the loss of nine killed and

12 wounded, out of a crew numbering 175, a portion of her complement having been sent away in charge of two American prizes.

On the 12th September the 28-gun frigate *Arrow*, Captain Portlock, and *Wolverine*, 13, Commander Bolton, found at anchor in the passage leading from Vlie Island to Harlingen, not far from the Texel, the Dutch ship *Draak*, of 24 guns, and 14-gun brig *Gier*, and while the latter struck to the *Wolverine* (lately commanded by the brave Mortlock, who fell in action) without firing a shot, the *Draak* prepared for resistance, lying with springs on her cables, so that her broadside fire was brought to bear on the *Arrow* as she worked up to windward towards her. It was twenty minutes before the British frigate could reply, but on approaching within eighty yards she opened fire, and in a quarter of an hour silenced the Dutchman.

The war gave numberless opportunities to young officers of an enterprising disposition to display their qualities, among whom was Mr. Michael Fitton, of the *Abergavenny*, stationary flag-ship at Jamaica, who, though he had seen over eighteen years' service, owing to want of interest or ill-fortune, had not risen above the rank of acting lieutenant. This officer took command of a boat of the *Abergavenny* in order to cruise off the island to pick up prizes, and, having been successful, soon found himself in charge of a prize schooner, named the *Ferret*, mounting six three-pounders, and a crew of 45 men and boys. With this little craft he engaged a large privateer schooner of 14 guns and 100 men, which made off; and though the *Ferret* again brought her to action that night, she escaped, being close to the port of San Jago, in Cuba ; but it was afterwards ascertained that her loss was 11 killed and 20 wounded—a surprising result from the fire of three-pounders.

About a twelvemonth later Acting-Lieutenant Fitton started on a cruise on the Spanish main in a tender of the *Abergavenny*, lately captured from the enemy, with 44 officers and men, and on the 23rd January, 1801, sighted and gave chase to the Spanish "garda costa," *Santa Maria*, of six guns and 60 men. Though having only one 12-pounder swivel gun Mr. Fitton could not resist the chance of a brush, and engaged her with such effect that the enemy sheered off, and, running towards the land, grounded on the beach. The indomitable British officer followed suit, when, after sustaining and returning her fire for some little time, he jumped overboard with his sword between his teeth, and, followed by the greater part of his crew, boarded, and after a stout resistance captured the *Santa Maria*. His loss in achieving this brilliant success was two killed and five wounded, and that of the enemy five and nine respectively, including her commander, who had both his hands carried away by a grape-shot.

Off Porto Rico the boats of the 18-gun sloop-of-war *Echo*, under the command of Lieutenant Napier (afterwards so well known at Acre and as Sir Charles Napier in the Baltic during the Russian war), captured a Spanish armed brig, and a few days later made a daring attack on the French privateer brig *Buonaparte*, carrying 12 guns and 30 seamen, though the pinnace and jollyboat under his command had only 16 men. In spite of the disparity of numbers and in face of the fire of three guns from the beach, which sank the pinnace, Lieutenant Napier carried the *Buonaparte* by boarding and brought her off.

A singular anecdote for which the naval historian Marshall is responsible attaches to the capture of the French privateer *Bordelais*, mounting 24 guns with a complement of 200 men, by the *Révolutionaire*, 38, Captain Twysden. The British frigate sighted and chased the enemy off the coast of Ireland, and after a chase of 114 miles the *Bordelais* hauled down her colours. She was a new ship launched at Bordeaux, and esteemed one of the fastest privateers preying on English commerce, but the strange coincidence alluded to was that both the captor and her prize were constructed by the same builder, who, at a dinner given to her officers on her return from the first cruise, spoke in the following terms, which proved prophetic :—" England has not a cruiser that will ever touch her except the *Révolutionaire*, and should she ever fall in with this frigate in blowy weather and be under her lee she will be taken." The *Bordelais* was added to the Navy under her own name, and her establishment was fixed at 24 guns and 195 men.

A sad catastrophe occurred in the East Indies during the year, of the same nature as had befallen the *Resistance*. The sloop-of-war *Trincomalee*, of 16 guns and 100 men, Commander Rowe, while cruising in the Straits of Babelmandeb, encountered the French privateer *Iphigénie*, 22, and a hardly contested action lasting two hours ensued. The combatants fell on board each other, when suddenly, as the French commander, trusting to his superior numbers, was about to board, the *Trincomalee* blew up alongside and every soul perished except two, and the sides of the *Iphigénie* being stove in she went down, carrying with her 115 officers and men, the survivors, to the number of about 30, saving themselves on pieces of wreck.

The varied nature of what the French call " fortune de guerre " is shown in the next incident I have to chronicle. As the 38-gun frigates *Naiad*, Captain Pierrepont, and *Ethalion*, Captain Young, were cruising off the coast of Spain, they discovered the two 34-gun Spanish frigates *Santa Brigida* and

Thetis, homeward-bound with a cargo of specie, and giving chase were promptly joined by the *Alcmène*, Captain Digby, and *Triton*, Captain Gore. The Spanish ships separated, but the *Thetis* soon surrendered to the *Ethalion*, and her consort, after a pursuit lasting two days and a brave resistance, struck to the three other British frigates, one of which, the *Triton*, while chasing struck on the rocks off the coast near the port of Muros, but was got off. The British squadron escorted their prizes to Plymouth, where the specie was landed, and thence removed in 60 artillery waggons under military and naval escort to London, and finally deposited in the vaults of the Bank of England. So valuable was the cargo of the Spanish frigates, mostly boxes of dollars and doubloons, that the share of prize money of each of the four captains was £40,730, of the lieutenants £5,091, of the midshipmen £791, and of each seaman and marine £182. This was fabulous wealth in the eyes of poor " Jack " and " Joe," and amusing stories are told of the manner, such as frying watches, &c., in which they got rid of their hard-earned prize money.

Captain Macnamara, commanding the 32-gun frigate *Cerberus*—a dashing seaman who, when in command of the *Southampton*, had showed the true spirit of the British naval officer—while cruising off the coast of Spain, found himself surrounded by five of the enemy's frigates, and the professional skill with which, while engaging some, he eluded all, was brilliant in the extreme. Captain Macnamara actually fell on board one of the frigates, and frequently while manœuvring was so closely beset, that he had an enemy on either side, and fired both broadsides at once.

In another quarter, off the island of St. Domingo, the 32-gun frigate *Solebay*, Captain Poyntz, discovering four French sail—the *Egyptien*, armed store-ship, of 20 guns and 137 men, corvette *Eole*, 20 guns and 107 men, brig *Levrier*, and schooner *Vengeur*, the whole squadron mounting 58 guns and manned with 430 hands—instead of seeking safety in flight, hung about the squadron, and, closing with them in succession, actually succeeded in capturing the whole, and one of them, the *Eole*, served for many years under the British flag as the 18-gun sloop-of-war *Nimrod*.

The *Racoon*, 18-gun brig, Commander Lloyd, while cruising in the Channel, observed the French privateer lugger *Intrépide*, 16, boarding a merchantman, and, giving chase, laid the *Racoon* alongside the enemy, which struck after a determined defence with the loss of 13 men. The 36-gun frigate *Glenmore*, Captain Duff, and *Aimable*, 32, Captain Raper, while in charge of a large convoy, found themselves in presence of the French frigate *Sirène*, 36, Commodore Renaud (who, in 1794, off Mauritius, when in com-

mand of the *Prudente*, did little to make a reputation
as a gallant officer), and an 18-gun corvette *Bergère*,
with a large merchantman, to which Captain Duff,
mistaking her for a man-of-war, gave chase, when she
surrendered and proved to be the Indiaman *Calcutta*. Meanwhile the *Aimable* chased the other
vessels and engaged them both in the most gallant
manner, and had her consort not been decoyed away
by the merchantman, it is most probable that both
the ships-of-war would have been captured. As it
was, Captain Raper singly pursued the enemy a distance of fifteen miles, exchanging shot with them,
when, finding himself unsupported, he returned to the
convoy.

Lieutenant Pengelley, commanding the cutter *Viper*
of 14 guns and 48 men, rendered good service during
the year, first in March, when he captured, after a smart
action, a Spanish 10-gun brig, and after, in December,
when he brought to close action, after a running fight
of an hour and a half, the French privateer *Furet*, of
14 guns and 57 men. The vessels were thus well
matched, but victory was achieved by Lieutenant
Pengelley, who received a wound, but inflicted a loss
of four killed and 12 wounded, including the commander and his first lieutenant. The record of British
successes in the last year of the century had a fitting
conclusion in the recapture of the British 10-gun
cutter *Lady Nelson*. This little craft had been taken

off Gibraltar Bay by some French privateers and gun-vessels, which were towing her into Algesiras, when Lord Keith, whose flag was flying on board the *Queen Charlotte*, despatched boats from her and the frigate *Emerald* to the cutter's assistance. Lieutenant Bainbridge, in the *Queen Charlotte's* barge, with 16 men, ran alongside the *Lady Nelson*, and boarding her after a sharp hand-to-hand conflict, recaptured the prize, taking 34 Frenchmen as prisoners, six or seven others having been killed or knocked overboard. The gallant Bainbridge was severely wounded on the head by a sword-cut, but he brought the cutter in triumph to Gibraltar. During the war few more brilliant affairs took place than this, which reminds us of Nelson's exploit at Cadiz, not far from Algesiras, when, in July two years before, he in his barge, with Captain Fremantle and only ten seamen, engaged the Spanish commodore, and after a desperate struggle killed 18 out of 26 men forming the crew of his boat, all the remainder being wounded !

CHAPTER V.

THE year 1800 is not remarkable for any great naval battle or frigate action, but it is memorable for two as brilliant cutting-out affairs as any told in this history, with the exception of that of the *Hermione,* and for the loss of the *Queen Charlotte,* flagship of Lord Keith, Commander-in-Chief in the Mediterranean, when no less than 673 perished, including Captain Todd and 33 officers, of whom 18 were midshipmen.

The first capture made during the year was that of

the French frigate *Pallas*, a fine new vessel mounting
46 guns and having a complement of 350, but she
surrendered to superior force after a gallant defence.
First attacked by the 16-gun ship-of-war *Fairy* and
18-gun brig *Harpy*, three other ships joined in the
chase, the *Loire*, *Danae*, and *Railleur*, so that it was
no disgrace to Captain Epron to yield his ship, which,
under her new name of *Pique*, there being a *Pallas*
in the Navy, was long a favourite frigate in the
service. The *Loire* alone was more than a match for
the *Pallas*, which during the long chase inflicted on
her adversaries considerable loss aloft, with 36 killed
and wounded, while she herself was so cut up that in
a squall on the following day all three of her masts
went over the side.

Only a few weeks after this a portion of the crew
of the *Danae* broke out into mutiny, incited by a
seaman who had been secretary to Parker at the
famous mutiny at the Nore two or three years before.
The captain, Lord Proby, and the master were
wounded while endeavouring to quell the *émeute*, and
the ship was taken to Camaret Bay, near Brest, where
she was surrendered to the French. The mutineers,
however, to their chagrin, were marched off to Dinan,
and the officers of the *Danae* were released on their
parole and proceeded to England.

The British 36-gun frigate *Nereide*, Captain Watkins, having sighted, pursued four large privateers

and, after a twelve hours' chase and a run of 123 miles, captured the *Vengeance*, of 18 guns and 174 men. The *Phœbe*, 36, Captain Barlow, also found an easy prey in the privateer *Heureux*, of 22 guns and 220 men, which, mistaking the British frigate for an Indiaman, only discovered her mistake when within musket-shot range and struck her colours, with the loss of 18 killed and 25 wounded. Commander Austen, of the 16-gun sloop-of-war *Peterel*, also made a capture of the *Ligurienne*, of 16 guns and 104 men, in the Bay of Marseilles, after a running fight lasting an hour and a half, during part of which time so close were they to the shore that the *Peterel* received the fire of a battery. Commander Austen a few months later, while attached to Sir Sidney Smith's squadron on the coast of Egypt, sighted a Turkish 80-gun ship ashore, and to prevent her being carried off by the French, to whom she had been surrendered, sent a party of men to board the ship, which, as she could not be brought off, was burnt.

The *Leviathan*, 74, bearing the flag of Admiral Duckworth, and the *Emerald*, 36, Captain Waller, while cruising off Cadiz, sighted twelve Spanish sail, convoyed by the 34-gun frigates *Carmen* and *Florentina*, when the Admiral threw out the signal for chase. The pursuit lasted all night, and on the following morning the British ships arrived within gun-shot range, and after a few broadsides the frigates surrendered. The *Emerald,* most judiciously handled by Captain Waller, also succeeded in securing four of the convoy, which were taken to Gibraltar. The enemy made a gallant resistance, the *Carmen* losing 10 killed and 16 wounded, and the *Florentina* 12 and 10 respectively. Both the ships were added to the Navy.

As usual many gallant boat attacks took place during this year, and one cutting-out affair was specially remarkable for its audacity and success. For some time four French frigates had been blockaded in the Port of Dunkirk, and a squadron was assembled to attempt their destruction, but contrary winds prevented the task from being undertaken. At length, on the evening of the 7th July, the sloop-of-war *Dart*, Commander Patrick Campbell, followed by two gun-brigs and four fireships with some cutters and small craft, entered Dunkirk roads, and soon after midnight was hailed by one of the four frigates, to whose question whence she came, Captain Campbell replied, "De Bordeaux," and to a further query about the convoy astern, gave as reply, "Je ne sais pas." This brief colloquy over the *Dart* was suffered to pass unobserved until she arrived abreast the innermost frigate but one, which opened fire, promptly returned by the *Dart* with a broadside of 15 double-shotted 32-pounder carronades, when, ranging ahead, Captain Campbell laid his ship alongside the *Désirée,* of 30 guns and 300 men, his bowsprit passing between her foremast and forestay. Instantly Lieutenant McDermot, at the head of a division of seamen and marines, boarded the frigate on the forecastle, and though wounded in the arm quickly overcame all resistance, and hailed to say he was master of the ship, but requested a reinforcement of men, as the enemy were rallying. Thereupon Lieutenant Pearce with a second party of men sprang on board, and after a brief conflict they drove the Frenchmen below, cut the frigate's cables, loosed her sails, and brought her out in triumph. In this dashing exploit, which only lasted a quarter of an hour, the British loss was 12 killed and wounded, and that of the *Désirée* about 100, including nearly all her officers. The fireships were all set aflame, but the three other frigates cutting their cables ran before the wind out of the roads and escaped, and the two brigs and smaller craft did their duty in engaging the French gunboats and made many prisoners. For his skill and daring Commander Campbell received post rank, and First Lieutenant McDermot was made Commander—an honour also well merited by Mr. Pearce, who assumed command of the prize when he was wounded.

As brilliant and successful was the cutting-out of the *Cerbère* by the crew of the 14-gun cutter *Viper*, commanded by acting Lieutenant Coghlan. While blockading Port Louis it occurred to this gallant young

officer that he might succeed in carrying off one of
the gun-vessels constantly moving about the entrance
to that port; and as his offer was accepted by Sir
Edward Pellew, he manned a cutter with 18 seamen,
and accompanied by Midshipman Paddon, and taking
two other boats from the *Viper* and *Amethyst*, proceeded to carry out the hazardous enterprise.   The
brig *Cerbère*, which he selected for the experiment,
had 87 men on board, but though in his ardour he
lost the assistance of the other boats, which were left
far astern, and notwithstanding that the enemy
discovered his approach and were fully prepared to
give him a warm reception, he pushed on regardless
of all obstacles and boarded the brig with his handful
of dare-devils.   Nothing but success could excuse
such a rash undertaking, but success he achieved, and
a halo of immortal glory rests on the brow of the
youthful hero.   The night was "dark as a wolf's
mouth," and though this may have been an advantage
in concealing his numerical inferiority, it was unfortunate for him personally, as, when heading his men
to board, he sprang into a trawl-net hung up to dry,
when he received a pike wound in the thigh, and with
his men was forced back into the boat.   Nothing
daunted by this repulse Lieutenant Coghlan again
boarded the *Cerbère* farther ahead, but a second time
overwhelming numbers told, and he and his brave
band were knocked overboard or driven back into the

cutter. A third time the intrepid officer returned to
the assault with undiminished audacity, and such
heroism at length achieved the reward it merited.
The *Cerbère* was carried with a loss to the enemy of
six killed and 20 wounded, including every officer
on board, his own loss being only one man killed and
eight wounded, among the latter himself in two
places and Mr. Midshipman Paddon in six.   The
other boats had now arrived, and with their aid the
prize was taken in tow.   For his gallantry Mr. Coghlan received confirmation of his rank as Lieutenant,
and Sir Edward Pellew presented him with a sword,
and wrote of him in the following terms to Lord St.
Vincent, then First Lord of the Admiralty :—" I trust
I shall stand excused by your lordship of so minute
a description, produced by my admiration of that
courage which, hand to hand, gave victory to a
handful of brave fellows over four times their number,
and of that skill which formed, conducted, and effected
so daring an enterprise."

Many brilliant boat expeditions took place during
the year, and one of the smartest was that in
Barcelona roads, when eight boats of the *Minotaur*
and *Niger*, under the command of Captain Hillyar,
cut out the *Esmeralda* and *Paz*, described as ships
mounting 32 guns and laden with stores.   Receiving
one ineffectual broadside from the *Esmeralda*, Captain Hillyar, after a brief struggle, carried the ship,

when the crew of the *Paz*, learning the fact by the
cheers of the British seamen, cut her cable, but in
spite of a heavy fire from four batteries she also was
soon boarded and captured. Eight boats from Sir
John Warren's squadron, under command of Lieutenant Burke of the *Renown*, were despatched to cut
out or destroy a convoy lying at St. Croix—a small
harbour within the Penmarck rocks. Favoured by
the darkness of the night the boats reached the spot
unobserved, and at daylight, under a heavy fire from
a battery of three armed vessels, captured and brought
out one gunboat, two *chasse-marées*, and eight merchantmen, the remainder of the 20 sail, laden with
provisions and wine for the fleet at Brest, escaping
capture by running upon the rocks. The next
service performed by the boats of the squadron ended
in disaster. Lieutenant Burke, with 192 officers and
men, boarded and after some resistance carried the
French ship *Thérèse*, of 20 guns, and three other
armed vessels, together with their convoy of 15 sail,
all of which, as they could not bring them off, were
destroyed. Unfortunately on their way from the
scene of this exploit—at the bottom of a bay in the
island of Noirmoutier—the boats grounded on some
sandbanks, and, the tide receding, in ten minutes were
left high and dry. Now they were exposed to the
fire from some forts and from 400 soldiers, and though
they secured a vessel in which to embark, and dragged

her for two miles through shoal water, they were
surrounded and 92 of the party were made prisoners.

Lieutenant Burke and the brave men under his
command soon after had their revenge, and he
received the promotion to the rank of Commander,
which he had well earned by many acts of gallantry.
The French privateer *Guêpe*, of 18 guns and 161
men, having run for protection into Vigo harbour, Sir
John Warren sent 20 boats from his squadron to make
the attempt to cut her out as she lay under the protection of some batteries. Lieutenant Burke left the
Renown soon after midnight, and on getting alongside the *Guêpe*, was received with cheers, the French
crew being quite prepared to give him a warm
reception. But nothing could resist the impetuous
valour of the British bluejackets, and in a quarter of
an hour from the time of coming alongside they were
in possession of the ship, with the loss of five killed
and 19 wounded, including Mr. Burke and two other
lieutenants ; that of the *Guêpe* being 25 and 40 respectively, among the mortally wounded being her
brave commander.

A singular capture was made at this time of a
French frigate by an Indiaman. Captain Bulteel, of
the *Belliqueux*, 74, when off the coast of Brazil with
an outward-bound convoy of merchantmen, sighted
the *Concorde*, 40, Commodore Landolphe, and 36-gun
frigates *Medée* and *Franchise*, when he gave chase to

the *Concorde*, which surrendered after a feeble resistance. In the meantime four of the Indiamen proceeded in pursuit of the other frigates, and after a long chase, says an account, Captain Meriton, of the *Exeter*, found himself alongside the *Medée*, when he ordered the French commander to strike, and that officer, fancying by the formidable appearance of the large Indiaman, with her double row of ports, that he was in the presence of a ship-of-the-line, hailed to say he surrendered. The captain, on being brought on board the *Exeter*, asked to whom he had the honour to deliver up his sword, when Captain Meriton drily replied " To a merchantman," on which the indignant officer begged to be allowed to return to his ship and fight the battle out. The Indiamen, it may be noted, were frigate-built ships, carrying 26 guns, with strong crews, but though their appearance was striking, they were no match for a frigate. Nevertheless, some instances are recorded in which the gallant commanders of these Indiamen maintained the unequal struggle when victory was impossible. A noted case is afforded by the action between the *Kent*, Captain Rivington, off the Sandheads at the entrance to the Hooghly, and the *Confiance*, of 22 guns and 250 men, commanded by the noted Captain Surcouf, whose name as a successful privateersman was a terror in the Eastern Seas. For one hour and three-quarters Captain Rivington maintained the conflict, gallantly

THE MAIN-DECK GUNS OF THE "SEINE" IN ACTION.

seconded by his crew of 90 seamen and 38 military passengers, but when he was shot through the head, and 13 others fell by his side, besides 44 wounded, the *Kent* surrendered.

Captain David Milne—the second lieutenant of the *Blanche* in her famous victory over the *Pique*—when in command of the 38-gun frigate *Seine* (taken, as already mentioned, in June of the preceding year), whilst cruising off the island of St. Domingo, sighted the *Vengeance*, Captain Pichot, and, after a chase lasting all day, shortly before midnight (the hour Captain Faulknor engaged the *Pique*), being close on the enemy's quarter, fired several broadsides at her. But Captain Pichot, though his ship was of considerably heavier weight of metal and carried 50 more men, seemed only anxious to escape, and when he had crippled the *Seine* aloft, fell astern. Having repaired damages, Captain Milne again overtook his pusillanimous foe, and at 8 o'clock the following morning the action was renewed, when, after continuing hotly for two hours and a half the *Vengeance*, having lost her foremast, mizen-mast, and main-topmast, was in no condition to make further resistance, and an officer hailed from the bowsprit-end to say she surrendered. Her loss was about 35 killed and 70 wounded, and that of the *Seine* her second lieutenant, a son of the gallant commander, and 12 men killed and three officers and 26 wounded. The *Ven-*

geance, whose only standing mast went over the side, with nine feet of water in the hold, was towed to Jamaica, but her hull was so irretrievably damaged with shot holes that, though purchased for the service, she was never able to put to sea.

A gallant performance was that by Lieutenant Beaufort (afterwards Admiral Sir Francis Beaufort, hydrographer to the Admiralty), who, with the boats of the 38-gun frigate *Phaeton*, cut out the Spanish ship *San Josef*, though lying under the protection of a battery near Malaga. After a long pull all night, at 5 A.M. on the morning of the 28th October, Lieutenant Beaufort boarded and carried the *San Josef*—a name already rendered so famous as that of the ship Nelson captured by boarding in the battle of St. Vincent. Lieutenants Beaufort and Campbell received several wounds, and midshipman Hamilton was shot through the thigh.

A brilliant capture was that made by the privateer brig *Rome*, of 10 guns and 54 men, under Mr. Godfrey, of the Spanish schooner *Santa Ritta*, of 12 guns and 85 men, after a close action lasting an hour and a half, the enemy being captured by boarding with the loss of 14 killed and 17 wounded. The *Gipsy*, Lieutenant Boger, tender to the *Leviathan*, also engaged and captured the ship *Quidproquo*, of eight guns and 98 men, of whom five, including her commander, were killed and 11 wounded. Lieutenant Bond, of the schooner *Netley*, captured some Spanish

privateers, and the boats of Sir Richard Strachan's
squadron, under Lieutenant Hennah, gallantly boarded
and destroyed a corvette which had run ashore off
the entrance of the Morbihan ; but a disaster befell
the armed brig *Admiral Pasley*, which, being attacked
in a calm off Ceuta by two Spanish gun-vessels, was
compelled to surrender, after being nearly cut to pieces,
with the loss of three killed and her commander
master, and eight men wounded.

The last action of the year we have to chronicle is
one very honourable to the British officers and seamen concerned.   Lieutenant Smith, commanding the
schooner *Milbrook*, having a crew of only 47 hands,
while becalmed off Oporto, descried the privateer
Bellone, of 32 guns and 250 men, and getting out his
sweeps, commenced to engage the enemy instead of
taking to flight.   After a fight of about two hours'
duration the *Milbrook's* spars, sails, and rigging were
cut to pieces, so that she became unmanageable, but
the *Bellone*, which had lost 20 killed and her first and
second captains, and 45 men wounded, having had
enough of it, took advantage of a light breeze that
sprang up and made sail, leaving the little schooner
the victor in one of the most unequal encounters of
the war.   Lieutenant Smith was promoted for his
audacious gallantry, and the English merchants at
Oporto presented him with a piece of plate.

The year 1801 was as fertile of frigate actions and

boat expeditions as its predecessor. Off Porto Ferrajo, in the Mediterranean, the *Pomone*, Captain Gower after a brief resistance, compelled the French frigate *Carrere* to haul down her colours ; but other ships were then coming up astern, and the *Succès*, which went aground, struck her colours without firing a shot to the *Minerve*, Captain Cockburn, who, leaving the *Phœnix* to take possession, gave chase to the *Bravoure*, forced her also ashore, where she became a wreck, while the former was brought off the rocks and purchased into the British Navy under her Anglicised name of *Success*.

The men of the *Melpomene*, some 96 all told, under the command of Lieutenant Dick, achieved a partial success and displayed the dogged valour forming so marked a trait of the British character. Embarking in their boats they proceeded to cut out from under a battery in Senegal an 18-gun brig and an armed schooner. It was a desperate service, and though two boats were sunk by the enemy's fire, the brig was boarded, and, after a severe conflict, carried, but the schooner, having cut her cable, ran for protection nearer the battery, and all attempts to reduce her failed. In taking the brig down the river she grounded, and Lieutenant Dick had to abandon his prize, which sank in the sand, his loss being 11 killed, including Lieutenants Palmer and Vyvian and Midshipman Main, and 18 wounded, among whom were four officers, out of 60 seamen and 35 of the African Corps engaged.

The *Mercury*, 28, Captain Rogers, captured without loss or resistance the French 20-gun corvette *Sans Pareille*, and in the West Indies a party of 30 men from the *Daphne, Cyane*, and *Hornet*, under Lieutenants Mackenzie and Peachey, embarking on board the tender *Garland*, cut out the French schooner *Eclair*, of four guns and 45 men, from under the protection of a battery—a gallant exploit not effected without some loss. Buonaparte, having patched a temporary peace with Germany, bent all his energies on the invasion of England, and our Government appointed Lord Nelson to the chief command of the defences afloat and ashore between Orfordness and Beachy Head. His lordship, having 30 vessels under his orders, hoisted his flag in the *Medusa*, 32, Captain Gore, and stood across to Boulogne, on the 3rd August, 1801, but little was effected by a bombardment of the French flotilla, and a distinct failure was the result of an attack by the armed boats of the squadron, formed into four divisions, under Captains Somerville, Parker, Cotgrave, and Jones. The boats put off from the *Medusa* at midnight on the 15th August, but the three that were enabled to deliver an attack were repulsed, the enemy being fully prepared, having the boarding netting up, with a total loss of 44 killed and 126 wounded. An attack at Etaples was more

M

successful, and Captain Rose, of the *Jamaica*, succeeded in bringing off three or four boats with small loss. During the year the 32-gun frigate *Success* was captured in the Mediterranean by Admiral Ganteaume's squadron, despatched by Buonaparte with reinforcements of 5,000 men to succour his Egyptian army, which Sir Ralph Abercromby was preparing to attack with a success that is historical, though he fell at the moment of victory at Alexandria. But Ganteaume, learning that Lord Keith was in force off the coast of Egypt, gave up the attempt and proceeded to Toulon. On the other hand, the 36-gun frigate *Dedaigneuse*, bound from Cayenne to Rochefort, struck to the British frigates *Sirius* and *Oiseau* after a running fight of forty-five minutes. An equally unsuccessful, but much more sanguinary, defence was made off Barbadoes by the French brig *Curieux*, of 18 guns and 168 men, against the lately captured 24-gun ship *Bordelais*, Captain Manby. After only half an hour's close action, her captain being mortally wounded, the *Curieux* hauled down her flag, with the loss of about 50 men, her decks, when boarded, being found to be " strewed from end to end with dead and dying," and some of the gallant captors, in making strenuous efforts to remove the wounded from the sinking ship, went down with her and them, among the number being Midshipmen Spence and Auckland. The 18-gun brig *Penguin*, Commander Mansel, was not equally successful in capturing a French privateer corvette, but she brought her to close action, and it was owing to the loss of her fore-topmast that the stranger was enabled to escape.

A brilliant victory was achieved by Captain Barlow, of the *Phœbe*, carrying 44 guns and 239 men, over the *Africaine*, of like force as to weight of metal, but having no less than 715 men on board, including 400 troops bound for Egypt. Captain Barlow descried the enemy off Ceuta on the 19th February, who, finding she could not escape, turned at bay, and an engagement at pistol-shot range commenced at eight o'clock in the evening. After sustaining for ninety minutes the fire of the *Phœbe*, the *Africaine* surrendered, but not till she had five feet of water in her hold, the greater number of her guns were dismounted, and her decks were cumbered with dead and wounded, for the slaughter had been unprecedented. In striking contrast was the loss sustained by the two ships, though the masts, sails, and rigging of the British frigate were in little better plight than her opponent ; for whereas the latter had only thirteen casualties, the *Africaine* had 200 killed, including Commodore Saulnier and a brigadier-general, and 143 wounded (the greater part of them stated to be mortally), among the number being three generals, six naval lieutenants, and seven military officers. Captain Barlow was knighted, and his first

lieutenant, who was wounded, received promotion.
The *Africaine*, renamed *Amelia*, was purchased into
the service, and long continued to bear with honour
the Union Jack.

The boats of the *Andromache* and *Cleopatra*,
under Captain Lawrie, off Cuba, attacked a convoy of
25 Spanish vessels under the protection of three
armed galleys, but on their arrival at midnight within
gun-shot were received with a destructive fire of
grape and musketry, and could only succeed in
bringing off one galley, with the heavy loss of nine
killed, including the first lieutenant of the *Andromache* (Taylor), one master's mate and a midshipman, and twelve wounded. In the Mahé Roads, in
the Seychelles group of islands, in the Indian Ocean,
the *Sibylle*, the conqueror of the *Forte*, now under
the command of Captain Adam, discovered the *Chiffonne*, of 36 guns and 296 men, and, anchoring
within 100 yards, engaged her as well as a shore
battery, consisting of four of the frigate's forecastle
guns. After sustaining the fire of the *Sibylle* for
half an hour the *Chiffonne* struck, when the battery
was abandoned, the enemy's loss being 23 killed and
30 wounded. The prize was added to the navy
under her own name.

The exploits of Lord Cochrane, as told in his
"Autobiography of a Seaman," form one of the most
romantic and extraordinary pages of naval history,

and among his most brilliant feats was the capture
of the Spanish 32-gun ship *Gamo* by the *Speedy*,
lately commanded by Captain Brenton, mounting 14
four-pounders, and having a crew of 54 hands. The
Gamo had been specially despatched to capture the
little brig, whose depredations on Spanish commerce
kept the littoral of Spain in a state of alarm, and
the *Gamo* being disguised, it was only when he was
close to her Lord Cochrane found that he was confronted by a man-of-war. To escape was impossible,
though, indeed, there was no wish of either the
British commander or his crew to avoid an encounter,
and a cannonade commenced; but at this the brig's
four-pounders were no match, however skilfully
worked, with the *Gamo's* heavy guns; and when three
of his men had been killed and five wounded, Lord
Cochrane determined to board as his only resource.
Running alongside he boarded with every available
man—about 40 altogether, and so impetuous and
irresistible was the assault, that he actually carried
the *Gamo*, which lost out of her crew of 274 seamen
and 45 marines her commander and 14 killed and
41 wounded. The victory achieved must be placed
on a level with the capture of the *Hermione* by Captain Hamilton, of the *Désirée* by Commander Campbell, and of the *Cerbère* by Lieutenant Coghlan, and,
we might add, with Nelson's exploit off Cadiz. Lord
Cochrane was deservedly made a post-captain, and

his first lieutenant, Mr. Parker, who had been severely wounded by a bullet and sword-cut, was promoted to commander.

On the 9th June, a month after the capture of the *Gamo*, Lord Cochrane, while cruising in company with the 18-gun brig *Kangaroo*, Commander Pulling, discovered a convoy lying close to the Tower of Oropesa, under the protection of a 20-gun ship and three gunboats, and resolved to attack. Accordingly the brigs came to an anchor within gun-shot, and, opening fire, after a brisk cannonade silenced and sank the squadron, and ultimately the fire of the tower was also reduced. The boats now succeeded in bringing off three vessels laden with wine and provisions, and the others were sunk. In the affair midshipman Taylor was killed and two lieutenants were wounded.

Quite as remarkable as the capture of the *Gamo* or the *Hermione* was the cutting-out of the corvette *Chevrette*, having on board 339 seamen and soldiers, moored in Camaret Bay, near Brest, in full view of the combined French and Spanish fleet, and under the protection of some batteries, and quite prepared to receive an enemy. On the night of the 21st July fifteen boats of the *Robust*, *Beaulieu*, and *Doris*, under Lieutenant Losack, with 280 officers and men, proceeded to undertake the desperate duty of bringing her out, while the French—relying on superior numbers and the protection of some redoubts and

batteries, as well as a gun-vessel, and having their guns
loaded to the muzzle with grape-shot—were so confident of repelling the assault that they hoisted the
Tricolour over the English ensign in bravado. While
on the way Lieutenant Losack, with his own and five
other boats, proceeded in chase of a look-out vessel,
and Lieutenant Keith Maxwell, of the *Beaulieu*, after
waiting some time for his return, as the night was
far advanced and he had yet six miles to pull,
resolved to proceed with the remaining nine boats,
whose united crews were only 180 men. Having
allocated to them their several duties of boarding,
cutting the *Chevrette's* cables, and loosing her sails,
Maxwell proceeded on his way, and on arriving
within hail was received with a heavy fire of grape
and musketry. Pushing on without firing a shot he
boarded on the starboard bow and quarter and port
bow, and a desperate conflict ensued, the enemy even
seeking to board the boats in return. But nothing
could resist the impetuosity and daring of the British
seamen, who, cutlass in hand, succeeded in making
good their footing on the corvette's deck; and while
the majority under the gallant Maxwell were fighting
against overwhelming odds, the men told off for the
duty sprang in the rigging, and making their way
along the yards loosed the corvette's sails, while others
cut the cable, and, a light breeze having sprung up
from the land, the *Chevrette* was under weigh, steered

by Henry Wallis, quartermaster of the *Beaulieu*, who, though severely wounded, stuck to his post until she was clear.   On seeing the sails fall and their ship in motion the Frenchmen lost heart, and while some leaped overboard, others sprang down below, and in five minutes the combat was over, and the *Chevrette* was a prize to the heroic band of British tars !

It was not until it was over that Lieutenant Losack arrived with the other six boats, and assumed command of the prize as senior officer.   In achieving this surprising success our loss was 11 killed, including Lieutenant Sinclair, of the Marines, and Mr. Midshipman Warren, and 57 wounded, among whom were two lieutenants (one, Burke by name, mortally), one master's mate, and three midshipmen.   The *Chevrette* had 92 killed, including her captain, two lieutenants, three midshipmen, and a military officer, and 62 wounded, of whom five were officers.   Altogether this exploit was so remarkable that one is lost in wonder at the audacity of its conception and the success of its execution.   Needless to say, Lieutenant Maxwell was promoted, as was also his senior, Mr. Losack, on a misconception that he was actually present at the capture.

The boats of the *Mercury* rendered good service at Ancona, but failed in bringing away the late British bomb-vessel *Bulldog*, lying at the Mole, which was afterwards taken at sea by the *Champion;* but at

Corunna the boats of the *Fisgard, Diamond,* and *Boadicea,* under Lieutenant Pipon (who was promoted), entering the harbour, carried off the new 20-gun ship *Neptuno,* a gunboat, and a merchantman, all moored close to some batteries which opened fire on them. Also the boats of the 18-gun brig *Lark,* under Lieutenant Pasley, cut out in Cuba the Spanish privateer *Esperanza,* of three guns and 45 men—a service performed in the most gallant manner on a dark night in spite of a heavy fire from the schooner, by which 14 were killed and wounded out of 32 engaged. Great credit was due to Commander George Collier, of the 18-gun sloop-of-war *Victor,* for the persistence with which he stuck to the 18-gun corvette *Fleche.* The first encounter took place on the 2nd September, but owing to her superior sailing and the damages aloft sustained by the *Victor,* the *Fleche* got away and entered Mahé harbour, the scene of the cutting-out of the *Chiffonne.* Warping his ship into the inner harbour, Captain Collier opened fire at midnight of the 6th and set her on fire. The 18-gun brig *Sylph,* Commander Dashwood, twice engaged a frigate, whose nationality and force was never ascertained, with an interval of two months between the actions, and on each occasion, after a brisk engagement, the enemy made sail, leaving the honours of war with her plucky antagonist, which, however, was much cut up aloft. Commander Dashwood was posted, as Lord St. Vincent's letter says, "for his meritorious conduct in both actions."

The record of the year's exploits includes a very gallant one by the hired brig, *Pasley*, of 16 guns and 54 men, commanded by Lieutenant Wooldridge. This officer engaged a 22-gun Spanish ship-of-war, which made off, and a few months afterwards encountered a privateer of 10 guns and 94 men, and after an hour's cannonade ran her on board, and lashing her bowsprit to his capstan, boarded her with his men and captured her, after a hand-to-hand conflict lasting a quarter of an hour. In this affair the *Pasley's* loss was the gunner and two seamen killed, and her commander (who was promoted for his gallantry), master (mortally), mate, and five men wounded. The privateer suffered more heavily, losing 20 killed, including her commander, first and second lieutenants, and three other officers and 13 wounded.

On the 1st October, 1801, peace was signed between Great Britain and France, and the definitive treaty was concluded at Amiens on the 25th March in the following year, when England agreed to restore most of her conquests, including those in the East and West Indies, and Malta (a stipulation which, however, was not effected before war again broke out), the Cape of Good Hope, and other Colonial possessions, including Malacca and the Spice Islands, England retaining Ceylon and Trinidad,

while Denmark, Sweden, and Spain regained their
settlements.   England and France, foreseeing a re-
newal of the struggle, employed their time, before
the declaration of war on the 18th May, 1803, in
straining every nerve to strengthen their fleets, and
the arsenals and dockyards of both countries rang
with the din of preparation.   On the day before the
declaration of war Admiral Cornwallis sailed with
the Channel fleet of 100 sail to blockade Brest, and
Lord Nelson with his flag in the *Victory* steered for
the Mediterranean to assume the chief command.
The invasion flotilla in all the French ports, from
Ostend to Cape la Hogue, was watched by a squadron, and frequent skirmishes occurred between the
British cruisers or their boats and the divisions of
gun-vessels.

On the day war was declared the first act of hostilities took place, when the *Doris*, 36, Captain
Pearson, captured the *Affronteur*, of 14 guns and
92 men, after a spirited resistance, in which she lost
her captain and 22 men ; and on the 28th May the
36-gun frigate *Franchise* surrendered to the *Minotaur*, 74.   A month later the French corvette *Bacchante*, of 18 guns and 200 men, was captured, after
a chase of eight hours, by the *Endymion*, 40, Captain Hon. Charles Paget ; and the *Mignonne*, corvette, of 16 guns, and 40-gun frigate *Creole*, struck
to the British squadron in the West Indies, and were

added to the Navy.   So was also the *Duquesne*,
74, which surrendered to the *Vanguard*, 74, and
Tartar, frigate, after the exchange of several shots.
On the other hand, they regained the 38-gun frigate
Minerve, Captain Jahleel Brenton, which grounded
at the entrance to the harbour of Cherbourg, and,
after sustaining the fire of the batteries and gun-
vessels for ten hours, was forced to surrender, when
her commander, one of the most gallant and successful officers in the navy, was detained a prisoner
in France for two and a-half years, and the survivors
of the crew for eleven years, till peace was signed
in 1814.

Two boats of the *Loire*, under Lieutenant Temple,
boarded, and, after a desperate resistance, carried off
the 10-gun brig *Venteux*, lying under some batteries, when all the French officers were killed or
wounded.   Lieutenant Temple was promoted for this
exploit, as also was Mr. Midshipman Brydges.   The
Racoon, 18, Commander Bissell, attacked the 10-gun
brig *Lodi*, lying off St. Domingo, and when she cut
her cables, pursued and compelled her to strike, and
a month later she chased and forced ashore on the
Cuban coast another 18-gun brig, the *Mutine*.   Not
long after the same enterprising officer gave chase to
a brig, schooner, and cutter, and captured them, the
brig having 180 troops on board, and the others
also being full of troops, who tried to board, but

were repulsed and forced to surrender, with the loss of about 40 killed and wounded.

We have told how the *Kent* Indiaman maintained a protracted but unsuccessful resistance against the *Confiance*. Equally disastrous, but not so sanguinary, was the action between the *Lord Nelson*, a ship of the East India Company, carrying 20 guns and 102 men, and the 34-gun privateer *Bellone*, having a crew of 260. For an hour and a-half the action continued, when the *Bellone*, getting alongside, carried her opponent by boarding. A fortnight later the prize crew of the *Lord Nelson* engaged the 18-gun brig *Seagull*, but Sir Edward Pellew's squadron coming up they surrendered to the *Colossus*.

Lieutenant Rowed, of the cutter *Sheerness*, of eight guns and 38 men, captured a *chasse-marée* near Brest, and the plucky way in which, with his boatswain and three men in a jolly-boat, he boarded her as the crew, having run her ashore, left her on the other side, and then repelled a boat with ten men, was above all praise, and forms another striking instance of that hardihood which distinguished our seamen during the great war. Equally gallant was the manner in which the cutter *Princess Augusta*, of eight guns and 26 men, engaged and beat off, after an hour's close engagement, two Dutch schooners, whose united force in guns and men was 20 and 120 respectively, but Lieutenant Scott paid for his suc-

cess with his life, his dying injunctions to the master
being to fight the cutter bravely, and tell Lord Keith
that he had done his duty.   The boats of the 16-
gun brig *Atalante*, under Lieutenant Hawkins and
Mr. Burstal, the master, carried in the most gallant
manner, under a heavy fire from soldiers on the
beach, two French vessels, Mr. Burstal and only
six men killing in the hand-to-hand encounter six
Frenchmen, when the rest were either thrown overboard or driven below.   In the same dare-devil
fashion Lieutenant Henderson, of the *Osprey*, with
only 17 men in a cutter, boarded and captured the
privateer schooner *Ressource*, having four guns and
43 hands, with a loss of 14 to the enemy, the
brave officer himself being wounded.

Heroic also was the conduct of Lieutenant Nicolls,
of the Marines, who, with only 12 sailors in the
cutter of the *Blanche*, on the night of 3rd November, boarded the French cutter *Albion*, having a
crew of 43 men, while lying at anchor off St. Domingo, and fully prepared to meet the attack.
Nicolls, the first man on board, was severely wounded
by the commander of the *Albion*, whom he shot
dead at the same moment, and the Frenchmen were
driven below.   The *Blanche* was fortunate in pos-
sessing an exceptionally gallant body of officers and
men, and two other feats of arms demand special
mention, one being so daring as to be almost in-

credible. Her launch, under Mr. Smith, master's
mate, with 28 men, boarded and carried, after an
obstinate conflict, a schooner having a crew of 30
Frenchmen, of whom six were put *hors de combat*,
and a day or two after Mr. Midshipman A'Court,
having been sent ashore to bring off sand in a boat
with eight men, sighted a schooner lying becalmed,
when the young middy, thinking it a fine opportunity
to do some fighting on his own account without
orders, pulled up astern, and, though two of his men
were wounded (one mortally) by the schooner's musketry fire, he actually boarded with the remaining
hands, and made a prize of a vessel having among
her passengers between 30 and 40 soldiers, commanded by a colonel who had bled under Buonaparte
at Arcola in his wonderful Italian campaign, and
who, when asked how he, a French colonel, could
surrender to a handful of Englishmen, replied, with a
shrug, that it was all owing to " le mal de mer," and
it would have been different had he been on shore !

The boats of the *Blenheim*, 74, under Commander
Ferris, of the 14-gun brig *Drake*, towed by her and
the cutter *Swift*, were successful in cutting out the
French privateer schooner *Hermione*, having 66 men
on board, of whom 16 were killed and wounded.
The party consisted of 134 seamen and Marines, of
whom the latter, numbering 60, were directed to
attack a nine-gun battery, while the blue-jackets

attempted to surprise the schooner.   The departure
from the *Blenheim* took place at 11 P.M., and so
judiciously was the expedition conducted, that both
parties arrived at their destinations at the same time,
and while the Marines surprised the battery, which
they blew up, the *Hermione*, which opened a fire on
the advancing boats, was carried with a rush in a
few minutes, the English loss being only half a dozen.
During the year 1803 the island of St. Lucia, in
the West Indies, was recaptured, the navy taking
a part in the operations, and all the Dutch colonies
of Demerara, Essequibo, and Berbice also changed
masters, and have since remained under the British
flag.   The French were also driven out of St. Domingo,
General Rochambeau's troops, who had embarked
on board the French ships, surrendering to Commodore Loring, when the 40-gun frigates *Sémillante*
and *Clorinde* were added to the British Navy, and
long performed good service under their new masters.

CHAPTER VI.

DURING the year 1804 several conflicts took place between our fleet of cruisers and gunboats under Lord Keith and Napoleon's invasion flotilla, consisting of no less than 1,339 gun-vessels and 954 transports, distributed among the ports of Ostend, Dunkirk, Calais, Ambleteuse, Etaples, and Boulogne, the latter, as being only about twelve leagues distant from Dover, being the principal rendezvous. A sad episode was the capture of the 18-gun brig *Vincejo*,

N

Commander Wright, who had greatly distinguished himself off the coast of Syria in the *Tigre*, under Sir Sidney Smith. The British brig was becalmed at the mouth of the river Morbihan, and being surrounded by a flotilla of 17 armed vessels, carrying 35 guns and over 700 men, made a protracted and gallant defence ; but when she was almost unrigged, with three of her guns dismounted, Commander Wright, who had done all a brave man could effect and was himself severely wounded, surrendered his ship to Lieutenant Tourneur, who, in accepting his sword, complimented him on the gallantry of his defence. Captain Wright was removed to the Temple prison in Paris, where he died under mysterious circumstances, though Napoleon strenuously disclaimed, and doubtless with truth, having offered violence to this brave but unfortunate officer. The British brig *Cruiser*, Commander Hancock, and *Rattler*, Commander Mason, engaged off Boulogne the Flushing flotilla, and captured one gun-vessel and drove a second ashore ; and Sir Sidney Smith with the *Antelope*, *Aimable*, Captain Bolton, and *Penelope*, Captain Broughton, forced several others ashore, the British loss being 13 killed and 32 wounded. Havre was bombarded, and at Boulogne, in presence of the Emperor, Captain Owen, of the *Immortalité*, with the *Leda* and three brigs, ran in and opened fire on some of the enemy's vessels that attempted to stand off from the land, and some

of these were stranded on the beach or grounded in
the heavy gale that was blowing, when upwards of
400 soldiers and seamen perished. On the 25th
and 26th August, probably to amuse Napoleon, who
had come down to Boulogne to distribute crosses on
his "name day," the 16th August, among the 80,000
troops forming the "grand army of invasion," a
division of 60 gun-brigs and 30 luggers (there
being 146 moored there), stood out to engage the
in-shore British squadron under Captain Owen ; but
the action was indecisive. An attack was also made
by four fireships upon the crowded harbour of Boulogne, but though these were all successfully exploded
the damage wrought was insignificant in extent. The
18-gun sloop-of-war *Albacore* drove on the coast of
Normandy five French luggers ; but on the other side
of the account the gun-brig *Conflict*, while engaging
with others the Ostend flotilla of 19 vessels which
had put to sea, grounded and fell into the hands of
the enemy.

A singular episode in the war in the West Indies
was the commissioning of the Diamond rock off Port
Royal Bay in Martinique by Commodore Hood, of the
Centaur, 74, who placed on its precipitous summit
five guns from his ship with 120 men, under the
command of Lieutenant Maurice. Four boats of the
same ship with 72 men, under Lieutenant Reynolds,
proceeded to cut out the brig *Curieux*, of 16 guns

and 70 men, lying under the guns of a fort in Port
Royal Harbour. Every precaution had been taken
to meet the apprehended attack, the guns being
loaded with grape and the boarding-netting triced up,
but, nevertheless, when the assault was delivered a
little before 1 A.M., after a pull of twenty miles, such
was the impetuosity of the seamen and marines, the
latter returning the musketry fire as the boats
advanced, that success crowned their efforts. Lieutenant Reynolds in the barge made for the brig's
stern, over which a rope ladder happened to be
hanging, and ascending by it to the taffrail, cut away
the tricing lines of the nettings, and was quickly
followed by his men, when a footing was obtained
on the deck. A desperate struggle ensued, but
nothing could resist their ardour, and the enemy
were driven back step by step to the forecastle or
down below, and in a few minutes all resistance
ceased, the sails were loosed, the cable cut, and the
brig was under way under a heavy fire from the
batteries. The gallant Reynolds received many
wounds, of which he succumbed, and Lieutenant
Bettesworth and Midshipman Tracy were also
wounded, while the enemy had 10 killed and 30
wounded, inclusive of all their officers but one. Few
more brilliant achievements are recorded in our naval
annals than the cutting out of the *Curieux.*

The schooner *Eclair,* Lieutenant Carr, of 12 guns

and 60 men, engaged a French privateer of 22 guns and 220 men, and so damaged her adversary that the latter made sail, when the *Eclair* stood in pursuit, though vainly. A month later Mr. Salmon, her master, with 12 officers and men, boarded and cut out the French privateer-schooner *Rose*, having a crew of 49 hands, of whom five were killed, and 10, including the commander, wounded—a gallant exploit indeed!

On the 14th February, off Porto Auro in the China Seas, Commodore Dance, of the East India Company's service, with 16 Indiamen and 11 " country" ships, encountered the *Marengo*, 74, Admiral Linois—who in May, 1794, had been captured by the *Swiftsure* when in command of the *Atalanta*, and two years later by the *Revolutionaire* when in command of the *Unité*—with the *Belle Poule*, 44, *Semillante*, 36, and *Berceau*, 16, and on the following day the British commodore engaged the enemy, when, after the cannonade had lasted three-quarters of an hour, the *Marengo* and her consorts ceased firing and stood away under all sail. Commodore Dance was knighted for his gallantry, and he and his officers and men were liberally rewarded by the East India Company and the Patriotic Fund for having saved property of such enormous value from falling into the hands of the enemy.

It is impossible to chronicle the numerous boat

attacks against the national enemy, and almost in every instance with success, but the boats of the *Drake* and *Emerald* did good service in the West Indies, and those of the *Penguin* off Senegal. Lieutenant Furber, with 50 men from the *Blenheim*, cut out the *Curieux* at St. Pierre, but owing to her being held fast by a chain, the party were exposed to a heavy fire from the shore, and had to quit the prize and return to the 74 with a loss of 25 killed, wounded, and missing.

Very gallant was Commander Younghusband, of the *Osprey*, of 16 guns and 120 men, in bringing to action the privateer *Egyptienne*, of 36 guns and 248 men, with a loss of 17, and to the enemy of 37, and so accurate was his fire that the privateer made sail; but it is gratifying to record that the fugitive fell in with the *Hippomanes*, 14, Commander Shipley, and after a chase of fifty-four hours and a long running fight hauled down her colours directly the sloop-of-war got alongside.   Not long after this the *Hippomanes*, under the command of Captain Kenneth Mackenzie, encountered the privateer *Buonaparte*, of 18 guns and 146 men, which, mistaking the late Dutch prize for a merchantman, bore down to the attack.   The ships falling on board each other, Captain Mackenzie called on his men to follow him, but only 18 obeyed, and when five had been killed and eight wounded, including the leader in fourteen places, nine made their way back to the ship, the remainder being made prisoners. The privateer displayed no inclination to renew the conflict and effected her escape.

Worthy of all honour, though not rewarded with success, was the defence made by the *Wolverine*, Commander Gordon, of 13 guns and 76 men, against the 30-gun privateer *Blonde*, having a crew of 240 hands. To give his convoy a chance of escape Commander Gordon engaged the enemy and maintained the combat for fifty minutes, when he struck his flag; but the French had little to boast of, as the *Wolverine* was so riddled with shot that she foundered. The *Wolverine* had a midshipman and four men killed and 10 wounded, and her gallant commander was promoted to post rank, though he languished for many years in a French prison.

As brilliant a feat as the cutting out of the *Curieux* was that of the Dutch brig *Atalante*, of 16 guns and 76 men, by five boats from the *Scorpion* and *Beaver*, carrying 60 officers and men, under charge of Commanders Pelly and Hardinge—a hero who met his death in action when in command of the *San Fiorenzo*. As he stepped on her deck Captain Hardinge found the enemy fully prepared to give him a warm reception, but nothing could resist the impetuous onslaught of the British tars, who emulated the example of their leader, who killed the first mate in a hand-to-hand encounter, but was himself cut down by the captain, who in turn was slain, and after a desperate struggle the Dutch were over-powered, and the *Atalante* became a British prize. Both Commanders Hardinge and Felly were posted, and Lieutenant Bluett was promoted, and seldom were honours better earned. Like a generous opponent Hardinge buried Captain Carp with the honours of war, firing three volleys over his body, and hoisted the Dutch colours while the ceremony lasted.

A hard-fought action was that between the *Wilhelmina*, Captain Henry Lambert, of 20 guns and 134 men, and the French 36-gun privateer, *Psyche*, having a complement of 250 hands. The engagement took place near Madras, but though the ships sighted each other on the 9th April, it was not until daybreak on the 11th that they actually engaged, when they were speedily locked yard-arm to yard-arm, but by 7 A.M. the *Psyche*, being much shattered and having lost her second captain and 10 men killed, and her commander and 32 wounded, made sail, leaving her adversary victorious, but in no condition to pursue. A desperate conflict was that between the *Lily*, Commander Compton, of 16 guns and 80 men, and the privateer *Dame Ambert* (late the packet *Marlborough*), having 60 more men, and it was this superiority which gave her the victory. Her guns being heavier the privateer disabled the *Lily* and then ran alongside, when eight attempts to board were repulsed, but on the ninth occasion Captain Compton and his

first lieutenant being slain, the colours were hauled
down, the greater portion of the *Lily's* crew having
fallen in the attempt to defend their ship, which was
renamed by her captors the *General Ernouf*, and fitted
out as a privateer. A desperate and sanguinary, but
unsuccessful, attempt was made to cut her out by the
boats of the *Galatea*, with 90 officers and men, under
the command of Lieutenant Hayman. It was, perhaps, a foolhardy adventure, for the enemy were fully
prepared and the batteries on shore were ready to
co-operate, while a schooner was moored athwart her
hawse to enfilade the assailants ; but with such examples as the *Chevrette* and *Curieux* nothing was
impossible. The fire was too deadly to overcome,
and only 25 returned to the frigate in an unwounded
state, among the slain being the gallant Hayman, and
out of the 26 officers and men forming the crew of
his barge, only three escaped death or wounds. It is
satisfactory to state that the quondam *Lily* did not
long fly the Tricolour, but blew up in an action with
the 18-gun sloop-of-war *Renard*, Commander Coghlan, the same heroic officer who cut out the *Cerbère*
with the boats of the *Viper*, and it is related of him
that the French captain, on running alongside, hailed
to ask if he would strike, when the British officer
replied, " Yes, and d—— hard, too," and soon reduced
the privateer to a sinking state and set her on fire,
when she blew up with the loss of over 100 men.

The boats of the *Tartar* cut out the schooner *Hirondelle* in the most gallant manner, and those of the *Narcissus, Seahorse,* and *Maidstone* experienced heavy loss in bringing out a craft from under the batteries in Hyères Bay. The *Loire,* Captain Maitland, captured the *Blonde,* of 30 guns and 240 men, the same privateer that had taken the *Wolverine,* and in the East Indies Admiral Linois, who had fled before Commodore Dance's fleet of Indiamen, displayed equal pusillanimity in not pressing home his attack on the *Centurion,* a 50-gun ship he found alone in Vizagapatam Roads.

The capture of four Spanish frigates homeward bound with specie from Monte Video brought on a war with that country. On the 3rd October the *Indefatigable,* 44, Captain Moore, *Medusa,* 32, Captain Gore, *Amphion,* 32, Captain Sutton, and *Lively,* 38, Captain Hammond, despatched by Admiral the Hon. A. Cochrane, under orders from the Admiralty, sighted off Cadiz the *Medea,* 40, and 34-gun frigates *Fama, Clara,* and *Mercedes,* when Captain Moore ordered the *Medea* to heave to, and sent a boat on board desiring him to surrender, but on her declining to comply an action commenced, though within half an hour all the four frigates struck after an honourable resistance, for they were greatly inferior in force to their adversaries. The *Clara,* which had been engaged by the *Amphion,* blew up, when 240 out of 280 on board her perished,

and the other frigates sustained a loss of 100 killed
and wounded. On the 12th November the King of
Spain declared war against this country, and until
Napoleon some three years later attempted to impose
his brother Joseph on the Spaniards as their king, we
found in "the Dons" implacable foes.

The naval events of 1805 were overshadowed by
the crowning victory of Trafalgar, but nevertheless
the year was not deficient in some brilliant frigate
actions and boat expeditions. Off Boulogne and the
other French ports some desultory operations took
place between the British squadron and the French
Invasion flotilla, but they were of an indecisive
character, and after Sir Robert Calder's action with
Villeneuve and the return of that unlucky admiral to
Cadiz with 29 French and Spanish sail, Napoleon
abandoned his projected invasion of England, and
before the end of August the grand army, under his
personal command, was making forced marches to the
Rhine. A brave but futile resistance against superior
force was made by the *Arrow*, of 28 guns and 132
men, and *Acheron*, bomb vessel, against two frigates
mounting 48 and 42 guns, with 1,300 seamen and
soldiers. They were convoying 34 merchantmen, of
whom only three were captured, and to save their
charge sacrificed themselves, for a successful resistance
was impossible. The *Arrow* lost 40 men and the
Acheron 11, and such was the condition to which they

were reduced before being surrendered by Commanders Vincent and Farquhar (who were both promoted for their gallantry) that the *Arrow* sank and the *Acheron* was set on fire by her captors. The next action we have to describe was fought out on equal terms, such advantage as there was being with the enemy. The brig *Curieux*, Commander Bettesworth, of 16 guns and 67 men, encountered the privateer *Dame Ernouf*, of the same weight of metal but carrying a crew of 120, and after the action had lasted forty minutes the privateer, finding her gunnery overmatched, ran on board, when her superior numbers would tell, but Commander Bettesworth manœuvred so as to keep her off, and sweeping her decks, shot away her foremast, when she surrendered with the loss of 30 killed and 40 wounded—a sufficient indication of the valour of the defence, the *Curieux* only losing five killed and her captain and a few wounded.

Captain Lambert, who, when commanding the *Wilhelmina*, had engaged the privateer *Psyche*, was fortunate enough, when captain of the 36-gun frigate *San Fiorenzo*, to encounter his old antagonist, now purchased into the French Navy, and commanded by Bergeret, one of its most daring officers. True, the British frigate was of superior force, but this did not always ensure a victory to the British. After a chase lasting forty hours, Captain Lambert got alongside the *Psyche* at 8 P.M., and a furious action ensued

HERBERT K. ROOKE.

"COMMANDER BETTESWORTH MANŒUVRED SO AS TO KEEP HER OFF, AND SWEEPING HER DECKS, SHOT AWAY HER FOREMAST."

at 100 yards' range until midnight, when she struck,
with the loss out of 240 of her second captain, both
her lieutenants, and 45 killed and 70 wounded, more
than half her crew, so that Captain Bergeret maintained his reputation as a brave officer, while the *San
Fiorenzo* had 12 killed, including Midshipman Lefroy,
and 36 wounded.   In this instance the defence was
even more honourable than the victory, as in that of
the *Arrow* and *Acheron* and so many cases we have
described.   A case in point occurs in the capture of
the British frigate *Cleopatra*, Sir Robert Laurie, by
the *Ville de Milan*, the relative broadside weight of
metal being 280 and 340 pounds, and the crews 200
and 350 men.   After a protracted chase and over
three hours' action in which, by the destruction of her
wheel and running rigging, the *Cleopatra* became
unmanageable, the French frigate bore up and ran
her on board, when a large party sprang on deck, and
the British frigate, which had lost 22 killed and 36
wounded, became a French prize.   Soon afterwards
her fore and main-masts went over the side, and the
bowsprit followed suit.   The *Ville de Milan* had 10
killed, including her captain, M. Renaud, but the
enemy derived no benefit from their hard-earned
victory, for the *Leander*, 50, Captain Talbot, sighted
the two ships in company a few days later and captured
them in succession—an easy task, as they were both
jury-rigged, each having lost two out of her three

masts in the action. It is an interesting circumstance that the late centenarian, Admiral of the Fleet Sir Provo Wallis, who served as second lieutenant of the *Shannon* in her memorable action with the *Chesapeake*, was a youngster on board the *Cleopatra*. Sir Robert Laurie was placed in command of the *Milan*, as she was called, and her first lieutenant, Balfour, was promoted.

It is impossible within the space at our command to particularise the boat actions and other gallant deeds of our Navy, so I will only mention the storming of a tower on the island of Cuba by Lieutenant Oliver, of the *Bacchante*, with 13 men, though held by 30 Spanish soldiers, for which he was promoted ; the gallantry of Midshipman Smith, commanding a tender to the *Hercule*, who drove ashore a schooner carrying seven guns and 96 men ; of the capture of a Spanish privateer by Lieutenant Prieur, who embarked in a shallop with 25 men, and disguising her, permitted the privateer to run alongside, when after a brief struggle he turned the tables on the enemy, which had to a man the same crew ; and above all the exploits of Lieutenant Yeo, first of the *Loire*, than whom the Navy never reared a braver officer. With two boats he first boarded and captured, near Cape Finisterre, a Spanish felucca, killing 19 out of her crew of 50 men, and, a few days later, landing with 50 seamen and marines, he stormed a battery and, pushing on, had the temerity to attack a fort, mounting 12 long 18-pounders which had inflicted severe loss on the frigate. Fortunately he found the water-gate open, and engaging the governor in a single combat Yeo killed him, and rapidly advancing put to flight the garrison, consisting of 120 men, Spanish soldiers and French seamen from the 24-gun privateer *Confiance*, and took possession of the fort. It was a surprising feat of arms, and that the resistance was not merely nominal was proved by the fact that 10 of the enemy, including the captain of the *Confiance*, were killed and 30 wounded. The gallant Yeo was promoted to commander and then to captain, and received command of the privateer.

Lieutenant Pigot, of the *Cambrian*, captured with her boats the Spanish privateer *Matilda*, of 14 guns and 60 men, and on her proceeding up the St. Mary's River—then forming the southern boundary of the United States—made prize of an armed ship and brig, though not without loss, Pigot being wounded in three places, and the enemy having 25 killed and 22 wounded. The *Blanche*, 36, Captain Mudge, made a protracted resistance against the *Topaze*, of equal force, and three corvettes, but the odds were too great for a successful defence, and after having her rigging cut to pieces, seven guns dismounted, and with six feet of water in the hold, the *Blanche* surrendered and soon after sank. The *Topaze* carried a crew of 340

men, besides 70 soldiers, to her 215, but the small
loss sustained by the French ship showed that the
gunnery of the British frigate was not what it should
have been. Soon after two of these corvettes, the
Faune and *Torche*, surrendered to the *Camilla* and
Goliath. The *Calcutta*, formerly an Indiaman, carrying 54 guns, was surrounded by the Rochefort
squadron, and after gallantly engaging the 40-gun
frigate *Armide*, and the 74, *Magnanime*, Captain
Woodriff, who had a convoy in charge, was fain to
strike, but not until his ship was almost unrigged.

In the East Indies Admiral Linois, after his engagement with the *Centurion*, sailed for Mauritius to refit,
and proceeding to sea with the *Marengo*, 80, and
Belle Poule, 44, captured the *Brunswick*, Indiaman,
and while on his way to the Cape of Good Hope
encountered the *Blenheim*, 74, bearing the flag of Sir
Thomas Troubridge (which not long after foundered
at sea with all hands), who had come out to relieve Sir
Edward Pellew in command of the East India station,
but after an ineffective cannonade bore up, when
Troubridge pursued his course to Madras with his
convoy. At St. Simon's Bay Linois was joined by
the *Atalante* (which soon after went ashore and was
lost) and made the best of his way home. But neither
the *Marengo* nor the *Belle Poule* were destined to
reach *la belle France*, for in March, 1806, just three
years after leaving Brest, Linois encountered off that

port the line-of-battle ships *London* and *Foudroyant*, and while the *Marengo* after a gallant resistance struck to the *London* with the loss of 63 killed and 80 wounded, including the admiral and Captain Vrignaud, the *Belle Poule* surrendered to the 38-gun frigate *Amazon*, Captain William Parker (who commanded in the China war in 1840), one of our finest frigate captains. The resistance made by the *Marengo* and *Belle Poule*, and the victory achieved by Sir Harry Neale and Captain Parker, were most creditable, though doubtless both gallant officers wished that the *Foudroyant* had not been present to share with them the honours. The 36-gun frigate *Sémillante*, which Linois had sent to the Philippine Islands, while lying under the protection of some batteries, was attacked by the *Phaeton*, 38, Captain Wood, and *Harrier*, 18, Commander Ratsey, but finding it was impossible to capture her or silence her fire and that of the forts, they hauled off.

One of the bravest officers in the British navy was Captain Thomas Baker, who at this time was in command of the 36-gun frigate *Phœnix*, and he gave a brilliant proof of this in his capture of a French frigate of superior force, the *Didon*, which carried 85 more men and threw a far heavier broadside, and was, moreover, commanded by Captain Milius, one of the best officers in the French Marine. With all these advantages the *Didon* became a prize to her

O

foe. The action was fought under a press of canvas, at pistol-shot range, and was of a very determined character, the ships lying yard-arm to yard-arm, and when the ensign of the British frigate was shot away it actually fell on board the *Didon*. But in rapidity of firing and smart manœuvring the *Phœnix* was the superior, though both frigates were much cut up aloft, their sails hanging in ribbons from the yards. After a brief suspension of hostilities, employed in refitting, the *Phœnix* made sail after her adversary, and taking up a position on her bow, was about to re-open fire, when the *Didon* struck, three hours and a half after the action commenced. Of 245 men the *Phœnix* lost her second lieutenant, master's mate, and 10 killed and 28 wounded, including three officers, and the *Didon* had 27 killed and 44 wounded, out of a crew numbering 330. Taking in tow his prize, whose mainmast had to be cut away, Captain Baker stood for Plymouth, where, after narrowly escaping capture by Villeneuve's fleet, he anchored twenty-four days after the action.

The 26-gun corvette *Cyane*, late of the British service, was captured by the *Princess Charlotte*, 36, after a gallant resistance, and her consort, the *Naiad*, of 20 guns, which fled without affording her assistance, gained nothing by her pusillanimous conduct, as she was taken a week later by the *Jason*, 32, after a long chase and feeble resistance. The French

38-gun frigate, *Libre*, also surrendered to the *Loire* and *Egyptienne*, having made a gallant fight of it, as was proved by all her masts going over the side, in which condition she was towed by the *Loire* to Plymouth.

The year 1806 was heralded by a brilliant exploit, the capture of the Spanish brig *Raposa*, of 12 guns and 75 men, by three boats of the *Franchise*, commanded by Lieutenants Fleming and Douglas, with small loss to the victors, but of 31 to the vanquished. Lieutenant Ussher, of the brig *Colpoys*, distinguished himself by capturing three Spanish luggers, which he did with one of three boats commanded by himself, though the odds must have been six to one, for which he received his promotion. The *Pique*, 36, Captain Ross, engaged the brigs *Phaeton* and *Voltigeur*, of 16 guns and 115 men each, and captured them both, but she lost her master and eight men killed and three lieutenants, and 11 wounded, owing to her having placed a party of 25 on board one of the brigs, who were overpowered until more men were sent in a boat. The prizes were commissioned as the *Mignonne* and *Musette*. The *Renommée* brought off from under some batteries the *Vigilante*, of 18 guns and 109 men, and her boats, under Sir William Parker, cut out a schooner, and later a Spanish tartan, under a heavy fire. The boats of the *Pallas*, Lord Cochrane, also carried the French corvette

Tapageuse, of 14 guns and 95 men, and his lordship
chased and drove ashore two 20-gun corvettes and a
16-gun brig. The *Pallas* soon after stood into the
Roads of Aix, when the *Minerve,* 40, and three brigs
stood out to meet her, and an engagement ensued, in
the course of which Lord Cochrane, being fearful the
frigate would escape him, though she was double his
size, ran her on board, when his fore-topmast and
jibboom went over the side, and the shock of the
collision caused the frigates to separate. The French
admiral off the isle of Aix, seeing that the *Minerve*
had lost her foreyard, sent two frigates to her assistance, when Lord Cochrane made what sail he could.

  Captain Prowse, of the *Sirius,* gallantly engaged
off the Tiber a flotilla, carrying 97 guns, and captured
the *Bergere,* of 18 guns and 190 men, but lost nine
killed and 20 wounded in the unequal conflict. The
French 16-gun brig corvette, *Diligente,* surrendered
without firing a shot to the sloop-of-war *Renard,*
18, Commander Coghlan—a marked contrast, and one
characteristic of British and French seamen, to the
conduct of the Indiaman, *Warren Hastings,* which,
though a merchantman and carrying only 36 guns and
138 men, resisted long and gallantly the *Piemontaise,*
of 46 guns and 385 hands, though Captain Larkins
knew success was impossible with such disparity of
force.   What resulted from an equality was proved
when within a month the *Blanche,* Captain Lavie,

having 46 guns and 265 men, captured with trifling loss the *Guerrière*, of 50 guns and 330 hands, which had 20 killed and 30 wounded. Captain Lavie was knighted, and his first lieutenant, Davies, received promotion, but a sad fate attended the prize, which was taken a few years later by the American frigate *Constitution*. The *Greyhound*, 32, Captain Elphinstone, and *Harrier*, 18, Commander Troubridge, engaged the Dutch 36-gun frigate *Pallas*, and two other armed ships, and captured them all, while Captain Oliver, of the *Mars*, 74, did not hesitate to face four French frigates, one of which, the *Rhin*, of 40 guns, struck her colours.

The boats of a squadron off Rochefort cut out the *Cæsar*, of 16 guns and 86 men, after a gallant resistance, with a loss to the British of 48 killed and wounded, including Lieutenant Sibly in command, who was promoted. The *Arethusa*, 38, Captain Charles Brisbane, and *Anson*, 44, Captain Lydiard, having driven the 34-gun frigate *Pomona* to take shelter near Havana, stood within pistol-shot of a fort mounting eleven 36-pounders, and engaging it as well as the frigate and 10 gun-boats, drove ashore, sunk, or destroyed the latter, forced the *Pomona* to strike her colours in 35 minutes, and silenced the fort, with the loss of 34 on board the "Saucy" *Arethusa*, including her captain among the wounded. The *Pomona*, which was added to the navy as the *Cuba*, had her commander and 20 men killed, and 32 officers and men wounded. A very gallant defence was made by the French 40-gun frigates *Gloire*, *Indéfatigable*, *Armide*, and *Minerve* (the last the one engaged by Lord Cochrane), against the squadron blockading Rochefort, under Sir Samuel Hood, but it failed to prevent their capture, though, says the British Commodore (who lost his arm in the action), " their obstinate resistance was attended with much slaughter." They were all added to the navy, the name of the *Gloire* being changed to *Alceste*, and of the *Indéfatigable* to *Immortalité*. So also was another frigate, the *Présidente*, of 44 guns and 330 men, which surrendered to a second British squadron. Off the Java coast Captain Rainier, of the *Caroline*, 36, engaged a Dutch frigate of equal force and captured her, but the prize, though added to the navy as the *Java*, proved no acquisition, as she foundered with all hands in company with the *Blenheim*. The year was closed with the capture, after a chase of 67 hours and a spirited action, of the privateer *Superbe*, of superior force, by the *Pitt*, schooner, Lieutenant Fitton, in command, an officer whose name has before figured in these pages.

The year 1807 commenced with a very gallant exploit—the cutting-out, after a seven hours' pull, of the French brig *Lynx*, having 16 guns and 161 men, by five boats from the *Galatea*, with 75 officers

and men, under the command of her First Lieutenant,
Coombe, who had before lost a leg in action. Not
even, perhaps, the cutting-out of the *Cerbère* or
Chevrette exceeded this affair in the desperate valour
displayed by the British, whose loss was nine killed
and 22 wounded, including the gallant Coombe.
Twice were they repulsed, when the boats dropped
astern, and after pouring through the brig's quarter
ports a destructive musketry fire, again dashed alongside and gained her deck, the Second Lieutenant,
Walker, falling dead of his third wound. But in
five minutes all was over, and the crew were either
hors de combat or driven aloft or down below, their
loss being a lieutenant and 13 men killed, and
the captain, first lieutenant, four other officers, and
14 wounded. The gallant Coombe was promoted
and placed in command of the prize, which received
the name of *Heureux*, there being a *Lynx* in the
service.

The boats of the *Lark*, under Commander Nicholson,
boarded and carried a Spanish gunboat, but not without loss, he himself being among the wounded ; and
those of the *Bacchante*, Commander Wise, stormed a
fort in St. Domingo with 18 casualties, and of the
Comus, under Lieutenant Watts, who was severely
wounded, cut out a Spanish felucca from under some
batteries. The *Jason*, Captain Thomas Cochrane, recaptured the British sloop-of-war *Favourite*, of 29

guns and 150 men; and a prize schooner, under Lieutenant Hall, with 25 men, attacked the Spanish privateer *Mercedes*, having a crew of 30 hands, and running alongside, forced her to surrender after a determined struggle. On the other hand, the boats of the *Spartan*, Captain Jahleel Brenton, met with a sanguinary repulse off Nice. She had been chasing a polacre ship all day, and being becalmed at a distance of five miles, Captain Brenton sent his two senior lieutenants, Weir and Williams, with 70 men, who met with an unexpected resistance. Instead of being a merchantman she proved to be an armed ship prepared at every point for defence, with boarding nettings triced up. As the boats pulled alongside in two divisions, before even they could board, so heavy a fire of musketry and cannon was opened on them, that only seven men out of the 70 engaged escaped unscathed, among the killed or mortally wounded being both lieutenants. The survivors pulled back to the *Spartan*, which soon after had a narrow escape from being captured by a French 74 and two frigates. Captain Brenton was not an officer to be cowed by repulse, and he had his revenge at Naples three years later, when single-handed he engaged the *Ceres*, of 42 guns and 320 men, and *Fama*, corvette, of 22 guns and 220 hands, with a brig, cutter, and seven gunboats, the whole having 95 guns and 1,400 men to his 46 guns and 258 sailors. The *Spartan* first engaged the frigate, into which she poured a treble-shotted broadside, inflicting great carnage in her crowded decks, where the seamen and troops were drawn up in readiness to board, and passing on, discharged broadsides into the corvette and brig. A heavy fire was now opened on her from every side, especially from the long 18-pounders of the gunboats, as the wind had died away, and Captain Brenton fell severely wounded, when Lieutenant Willes continued the action, and ultimately drove off the squadron, capturing the brig. In this brilliant affair the *Spartan* had 10 seamen killed and 22 wounded, and the French acknowledged to a loss of 30 killed and 190 wounded, including the first and second captains of the *Ceres*, which was exclusive of that sustained by the captured brig. Some little time before this the *Ceres* had been engaged by the *Cyane* of 30 guns and 175 men, and nothing could exceed the gallantry with which Commander Staines at pistolshot range attacked so superior an enemy. The *Cyane*, however, suffered severely, being almost reduced to the condition of a wreck, while the captain and First Lieutenant, Hall, were both dangerously wounded.

The boats of the *Hydra*, manned with 50 sailors and marines, under Lieutenant Drury, first landed and stormed a fort on the coast of Catalonia, and seizing the boats on the beach, Drury boarded three heavily armed craft, and having re-embarked his marines, warped them out under a fire from the beach. The gallant officer received well-earned promotion for his skilful management of the affair. Equally successful were the boats of the *Confiance* on the coast of Portugal, where they cut out a privateer; of the *Clyde*, in carrying off a sloop from under a battery near Fecamp; of the *Porcupine*, under Lieutenant Price, in the Adriatic, which cut out a Venetian gunboat moored to the shore, and a few weeks later performed other services of a like character; of the *Herald*, led by Lieutenant Foreman, also in the Adriatic, which brought off the privateer *Cæsar*; and of the *Renommée* and *Grasshopper*, under Lieutenant Webster, which boarded two French and Spanish vessels near Carthagena. The *Grasshopper*, Commander Searle, an indefatigable officer, also captured, after a running fight, the brig-of-war *San Josef*, of 12 guns and 100 men; and Commander Clavell, of the *Weasel*, of 18 guns and 120 men, made a clever capture off Corfu of transports conveying 270 French soldiers as a reinforcement for the garrison, and took them all to Malta.

A brilliant achievement was that of the packet *Windsor Castle*, Commander Rogers, of eight guns and 28 men, which turned the tables on the French privateer *Jeune Richard*, with a crew of no less than

92. Captain Rogers at first tried to escape, but finding that impossible, returned the fire of the privateer, which ran alongside and attempted to board, but was repulsed. A second attempt was also defeated, when the gallant Rogers sprang on the privateer's deck, and driving the crew from their quarters, made her his prize, with a loss of three killed and 10 wounded, nearly half his complement, that of the enemy being no less than 21 slain and 33 wounded. No better proof was ever afforded of the superior valour of British seamen than this remarkable feat of arms, which sheds a lustre on every man and boy on board the packet, and chiefly on the heroic commander. Not so successful was Commander Sheriff, of the brig *Curieux*, of 18 guns and 100 men, in a desperate action with the French privateer *Revanche* (late the *British Tar*), of 25 guns and 200 men. After a heavy cannonade the privateer ran on board and tried to capture the brig by a *coup-de-main*, but the attempt failed, and the two ships parted. The firing was renewed, but at length the *Revanche* made sail, leaving the *Curieux* in no condition to pursue. In this action against greatly superior force the brig lost her captain and 7 killed and 14 wounded.

Our review of this year's exploits concludes with the capture of Curaçoa, a Dutch possession in the West Indies, by the 38-gun frigates *Arethusa*, Captain C. Brisbane, *Latona*, Captain Wood, and *Fisgard*,

Captain Bolton, and the *Anson*, 44, Captain Lydiard. Standing in at daylight on New Year's Day, the squadron opened fire on the Dutch forts and 36-gun frigate *Halstaar*, and 20-gun corvette *Surinam*, the jibboom of the *Arethusa* being actually over the wall of the town. After firing three broadsides, Brisbane boarded and captured the frigate, and a party of the *Anson's* men took possession of the corvette, when Brisbane and Lydiard landed and stormed Fort. Amsterdam, though garrisoned by 275 soldiers. Fire was then opened on Fort Republique, and 300 seamen being landed to make an attack on the rear, it also surrendered, and by noon the town and island of Curaçoa were in the hands of the British, with the merely nominal loss of three killed and 14 wounded, that of the enemy exceeding 200. Captain Brisbane was knighted, and he and the other captains received gold medals commemorative of the action, while Lieutenants Parish and Sullivan, of the *Arethusa* and *Anson*, were promoted.

CHAPTER VII.

CAPTAIN NICHOLAS HARDINGE, brother of Field-Marshal Lord Hardinge, who had displayed such gallantry in the capture of the *Atalante*, died a hero's death while engaging a superior enemy. He was in command of the *San Fiorenzo*, 36, when he chased between Ceylon and Bombay the *Piemontaise*, 40, which had captured the Indiaman *Warren Hastings* after a gallant resistance, and shortly before midnight ranged alongside the enemy and opened fire; the

French frigate, however, got away, but two days later he overhauled her again, and at 6.20 A.M. the action recommenced. The cannonade continued for two hours, when, having greatly crippled her adversary aloft, the *Piemontaise* made sail before the wind and disappeared. Having repaired damages, Captain Hardinge continued in pursuit, and sighted her at daylight, when, finding an engagement unavoidable, owing to the superior fleetness of the British frigate, the enemy, for the third time, at four o'clock opened fire. In the second broadside a grape-shot killed the noble Hardinge, when Lieutenant Dawson assumed command, and the battle continued with the utmost fury till 5.49, when the *Piemontaise*—having her masts so shattered that they went over the side, and her rigging and sails cut to pieces, with 48 killed and 112 wounded out of 566 on board, including 200 Lascars —struck her colours. The British loss during the three days' action was 13 killed and 25 wounded, her crew mustering only 186, owing to sickness and the absence of many men in prizes. It was a brilliant victory, but was dimmed by the death of the heroic Hardinge, to whose remains General Maitland, Governor of Ceylon, gave the honours of a military funeral, and published a General Order adverting to his singular merit.

A gallant exploit was that of Lieutenants Bertram and Smith, with the boats of the *Emerald*, on the

coast of Spain, when, landing, the British tars captured
two forts mounting thirteen 24-pounders, and set fire
to an 8-gun schooner which they could not bring off,
but the brave fellows suffered the loss of nine killed and
15 wounded, including Bertram and three other officers. The *Childers*, of 14 guns and 68 men, engaged
the Danish brig *Longen*, carrying 18 guns and 160
men, when Commander Dillon was severely wounded,
but received promotion for his gallantry; but the
Seagull was captured by the same Danish brig, reinforced by six gunboats, after a desperate resistance,
during which she had Lieutenant White, her master,
and six men killed, and her captain and first lieutenant (both severely) and 18 wounded. Commander Cathcart was also promoted for his valour,
which was none the less meritorious because it was
unsuccessful. On the other hand, the *Stately* and
Nassau, of 64 guns, captured a Danish 74 after a
stubborn defence, in which she had 55 killed and 88
wounded. Many other actions deserving notice took
place with the Danes, including the *Tartar's* daring
attempt on the town of Bergen, when Commander
Bettesworth and Midshipman Fitzhugh were killed,
and the capture by the *Virginie*, 38, Captain Brace,
of the *Guelderland*, after a very gallant resistance, in
which her bowsprit and three masts were shot away,
and she experienced a loss of 25 killed and 50
wounded, including her commander.

The boats of the *Alceste*, *Mercury*, and *Grass-hopper*, under Lieutenant Stewart, performed excellent service in cutting out seven craft from under the Spanish batteries at Rota, near Cadiz, and those of the *Nymphe* and *Blossom*, under their Captains, Shipley and Pigot, made a daring though unsuccessful attempt to bring out from the Tagus (Portugal then being in the occupation of the French) the brig *Garrota*, of 20 guns and 150 men, in which the gallant Shipley was killed. A rare triumph on the part of the French was also achieved when the 18-gun brig *Carnation* struck to the *Palinure*, of rather less force, but not until Commander Gregory and all his officers had been killed or wounded, the boatswain being in command, who made a brave attempt to stem the French boarders. The *Palinure* was captured a fortnight later by the *Pompée*, 74. As for the men who had failed to back up the boatswain, 32 of them were tried, when a sergeant of Marines was hanged and 14 were transported to Botany Bay for cowardice. About this time Commander Coombe, of the *Heureux* (late *Lynx*, which he had captured), was killed by a shot from a shore battery, after he had boarded and taken a schooner with a crew of 39 men, his barge having only 19, and the last words of this hero, who had lost a leg in his country's service, were, " I die content ; I die for my country."

The *Seahorse*, Captain Stewart, was victor in one of the most sanguinary frigate actions on record. This was with the Turkish ship *Badere-Zuffer*, carrying 52 guns and 543 men, the British frigate having 10 less guns, and a crew at this time of 251 hands all told. There was also a smaller Turkish frigate, but she quitted the scene of conflict after receiving a few broadsides, and the *Seahorse* turned her undivided attention on the larger ship, which twice strove to board, but though the rigging of the ships got entangled, Captain Stewart manœuvred so as to avoid this, and after the action had lasted all night, the fire of the enemy, which had lost her mizen-mast and fore and main-topsails, ceased at 1.15 A.M. A boat was sent on board at daylight to take possession, when it was found that the Turkish frigate had lost 170 killed and 200 wounded, while the *Seahorse*, in achieving this remarkable triumph of good gunnery, had only fifteen casualties.

The *Sémillante*, carrying 40 guns and 300 men, committed enormous depredations on British commerce in the Indian Ocean, but her captain, Motard, consistently avoided engaging a British frigate until, in March, 1808, she was brought to action by the *Terpsichore*, having only 28 guns and 180 men. Captain Montagu made every effort to capture her, and when the *Sémillante* crowded sail, chased her for five days, but the enemy threw overboard part of his

P

armament and escaped to Port Louis, thence setting sail for France, which was reached in safety in February, 1809. In the action the *Terpsichore*, owing chiefly to an explosion on board, lost a Lieutenant and 20 seamen killed, and 22 wounded. Off the same port a disaster befell Captain Woollcombe, of the *Laurel*, carrying 30 guns and a crew of 145, who engaged with great gallantry the *Cannonière*, of 48 guns and 420 men, including 70 soldiers, placed on board by the Governor of Mauritius with the object of boarding the little frigate (whose tonnage was 526 to 1,102 of the enemy), but against such overwhelming force the *Laurel*, after being almost unrigged, was fain to strike her colours.

Captain Michael Seymour, of the *Amethyst*, a member of a distinguished naval family, received a baronetcy for his capture of two French frigates of superior force. On the 10th November, at 9 P.M., he brought to action off Lorient the *Thetis*, mounting 44 guns to his 42, and engaged her alongside as they fell on board each other, all the time running before the wind. At one time it seemed as though the *Thetis* would escape, for she shot away the mizen-mast of the British frigate, but then her own mizen-mast fell over the side, which equalised matters. As a last resource the French Commander determined to board, when his superior numbers, 426 to 261, would tell, but a broadside of round shot and grape fired right into her stern did terrible execution, and after a close cannonade between the ships, which lay closely locked, the *Thetis* surrendered at twenty minutes past midnight. She was now wholly dismasted and had lost her captain and 134 officers, seamen, and soldiers (of whom she had 106 on board) killed and 102 wounded, while the *Amethyst* had Lieutenant Kendall, of the marines, and 18 men killed, and 51 wounded. On the 5th April of the following year (1809) Captain Seymour chased the *Niemen*, mounting two more guns than her former opponent, and at 11.30 that night fired the first gun, but it was not until two hours and a quarter later that she ranged close alongside and the fire waxed hot on both sides. At 2.45 A.M. the ships fell on board each other, but getting clear renewed the cannonade, when, after losing her mizen and main-topmasts, the *Niemen* at 3.30 ceased firing. Soon after her main-mast went over the side, that of the *Amethyst*, together with the mizen-mast, having already fallen overboard. At this time the *Arethusa* came on the scene and the *Niemen* struck to her, but the credit of the victory achieved by Captain Seymour was in no way detracted by this unlucky chance. Of her 222 officers and men the *Amethyst* had eight killed and two marine lieutenants and 35 seamen and marines wounded, and the loss of the *Niemen* was 47 and 73 respectively. Both the French frigates were added to the navy, the *Thetis* being renamed the

Brune, and Lieutenants Blennerhasset and Hill were promoted.

The boats of the *Circe* met with a sanguinary repulse from the corvette *Cigne,* losing 56 killed, wounded, and missing out of 68, but Captain Brenton, of the *Amaranthe,* gallantly boarded and captured her in the teeth of a heavy fire from some shore batteries to which the crew had fled. We will pass over with a bare mention the recapture, on the 1st July, 1809, of the *Manby,* of 12 guns and 94 men, by the brig *Onyx,* of slightly inferior force, for which Commander Gill and Lieutenant Garrett were both promoted; the surrender of the *Isis,* 22 (which became the *Rainbow*), to the 32-gun frigate *Aimable,* Captain Lord George Stuart; of the *Hebe* (renamed the *Ganymede*), of 20 guns and 160 men, to the *Loire,* Captain Schomberg; and of the 40-gun frigate *Topaze* to the *Jason,* Captain Maude, and *Cleopatra,* Captain Pechell, though the credit of her surrender is chiefly due to the latter ship. The *Topaze,* which had taken the *Blanche* in July, 1805, was added to the navy as the *Alcmene.*

A gallant and protracted resistance was made by the *Junon,* of 46 guns and 350 men, to the 38-gun frigates *Latona* and *Horatio,* Captains Pigot and Scott, assisted by two brigs, but being dismasted she was eventually compelled to strike with the loss of 130, including her gallant Commander, Captain Rousseau,

mortally wounded. In this affair the brunt of the
fighting fell to the lot of the *Horatio*, which, out of
270 hands, had Midshipman Gunter and six seamen
killed, and her captain, first lieutenant, and 31
wounded. The prize was added to the navy under
her own name. The *d'Haupoult*, 74, also surrendered
to a British squadron in the West Indies, but on the
other hand, the *Proserpine*, 32, was taken by the
40-gun frigates *Penelope* and *Pauline*, after making
a gallant but hopeless defence. Some more detailed
account is due to the gallantry and superior gunnery
displayed by the crew of the *Bonne Citoyenne*, 20,
Commander Mounsey, which captured, after a six-
hours' engagement, the *Furieuse*, of like force. Both
ships were greatly crippled by the heavy fire they had
maintained, the British sloop-of-war discharging no
less than 129 broadsides, but while her loss was
almost nominal, that of the enemy was 35 killed and
37 dangerously wounded, including her captain and
two lieutenants. The *Furieuse*, whose main and
mizen-masts went over the side, was refitted in mid-
Atlantic, and taken in tow by her victor, though only
half her tonnage (500 to 1,100) and almost equally
crippled, and brought in safety to Halifax at the end
of twenty-five days—a striking testimony to the sea-
manship of Captain Mounsey and his crew, who numbered, moreover, less than their effective prisoners.
The prize was purchased into the navy, and being

classed as a 36-gun frigate, was commissioned by
Commander Mounsey, now a post captain, his first
lieutenant, Symes, being also promoted.

Good service was rendered by the boats of the
Amphion near Trieste, and of the *Mercury* at Rovigno,
on the coast of Istria, while heavy fighting occurred
with Danish gunboats, the *Africa* and *Melpomene*
suffering severely when becalmed from the long 18-
pounders they carried. Conspicuous also was the
valour displayed by 270 seamen and marines, embarked in 17 boats from a British squadron under
Lieutenant Hawkey, First of the *Bellerophon*, despatched to cut out eight Russian gunboats. Of these
six were taken and one was sunk under a terrible
fire, the seamen boarding cutlass in hand, and 12
merchantmen under their protection were also taken,
but the gallant Hawkey and three other officers with
13 men were killed, and 37 wounded. Captain
Martin, of the *Implacable*, says of this officer—who
fell while in the act of boarding a gunboat, and died
with the words on his lips, " Hurrah, push on, England for ever ! "—" No praise from my pen can do
adequate justice to this lamented young man, as an
officer, active, correct, and zealous to the highest
degree ; the leader in every kind of enterprise, and
regardless of danger, he delighted in whatever could
tend to promote the glory of his country." The
Russian loss was very heavy, 63 being killed and over

50 of the prisoners wounded. Many more perished while attempting to reach the shore. On a second occasion, when three out of four gunboats were taken, the fighting was even more sanguinary, and 19 British seamen were killed, including three officers, and 51 wounded, among the number being Captain Forrest, of the *Prometheus*, in command, while the Russians lost heavily, and of the 44 men forming the crew of one gunboat every man was either slain or wounded.

A noble resistance was made by the *Junon*, 38, Captain Shortland, to the combined attack of the four French frigates, *Renommée* and *Clorinde*, of 40 guns, and *Loire* and *Seine* laden with troops. The former were on either side and the others ahead and astern, one with her bowsprit over the port quarter of the *Junon*, which, after she had sustained their fire for forty-five minutes and repulsed the boarders of the *Clorinde*, struck her colours. In this desperate defence of his ship Captain Shortland was mortally wounded, and 60 officers and men were stretched on the deck beside him, 20 of them being killed. So shattered was their prize that the victors, who acknowledged to a loss of 21 killed and 18 wounded, had to burn her. The *Loire* and *Seine* subsequently were taken by the *Blonde* and *Thetis*, while lying under the protection of two batteries on either side of a cove near Basse-terre, in Guadaloupe, and the batteries were stormed by a party from other ships, under Captain Cameron, of the *Hazard*, who was cut in two by a grape-shot, the British loss being nine killed and 22 wounded. Great havoc was wrought on our commerce in the East Indies by the French 40-gun frigates, *Venus*, *Manche*, *Bellone*, and *Caroline*, but the last-named, together with the *Streatham* and *Europe*, prizes, fell into the hands of Commodore Rowley when, in conjunction with some troops, he captured St. Paul's, in Réunion. During the year Senegal and Cayenne also fell to British arms, together with the important colony of Martinique, for his surrender of which Admiral Villaret-Joyeuse, Lord Howe's opponent on " the glorious 1st of June," was stripped of his rank and honours ; and in the following year (1810) Guadaloupe was taken, together with the Dutch possessions of Amboyna and Banda-Neira, and last, and most important of all, the island of Mauritius, the rendezvous of French cruisers and privateers. It is satisfactory also to note that two French prizes were recaptured—the *Laurel* by the *Unicorn*, and the *Confiance* (mentioned also in these pages as the *Cannonière*) by the *Valiant*, both on their return from Mauritius laden with valuable cargoes of colonial produce.

Many boat actions were fought during the year, almost always with unvarying success, but on one occasion the boats of the *Dreadnought*, in recapturing a Spanish trader from a French privateer, lost over 40

killed, wounded, and missing, and equally unfortunate
were the boats of a squadron at Palamos, on the coast
of Spain, where of 600 men, landed under Captain
Fane of the *Cambrian*, no less than 33 were killed
and 89 wounded, besides many made prisoners by a
strong body of French troops.   But victory in almost
every other instance crowned the efforts of our seamen, as well as in the numberless actions with privateers and ships-of-war of all classes from frigates to
schooners and luggers.   A very gallant defence was
made by the Indiamen *Ceylon*, *Windham*, and *Astell*
against the French frigates *Bellone*, *Minerve*, and
Victor, in which they lost 20 killed and 76 wounded
(including Captain Meriton, of the *Ceylon*, and his
chief mate, Mr. Oldham, severely), that of the enemy
being almost equal, and in killed even greater.   Captain Hope, of the *Astell*, which alone escaped, was
also wounded, and the officers and crew were rewarded
by the East India Company for their gallantry.
Captain Willoughby, of the *Nereide*, 36, made a successful descent on Jacolet, in Mauritius, and Réunion
(then called Isle Bourbon) was captured by the British
squadron in those seas, and also Isle de la Passe, off
Grand Port, in Mauritius (while in the possession of
the French), in which Lieutenant Norman, commanding, was killed.

But now a serious disaster befell the British squadron at Grand Port.   First the *Nereide*, overpowered

by the fire of the *Bellone* and *Victor*, was compelled
to surrender after losing, out of 281 seamen and
soldiers she had on board, her first lieutenant, three
other officers, and 88 men killed, and 137 wounded,
including Captain Willoughby (dangerously), the
second lieutenant, and five other officers, so that only
50 out of her entire crew remained untouched.
Commodore Duperré acknowledged to a loss of 37
killed and 112 wounded on board the *Bellone* and
Victor. Meantime the *Magicienne* had got aground
and Captain Curtis set her on fire to prevent her
falling into the hands of the enemy, and every effort
to get the *Sirius* afloat being vain, Captain Pym
destroyed her also; but Captain Lambert, of the
Iphigenia, succeeded in warping her clear of the batteries and of the fire of the other ships in port, but it
was only to fall a prey to four French frigates from
Port Louis, to which Captain Lambert had no choice
but to surrender both his ship and Isle de la Passe,
where he then lay. The ships were found at Mauritius
upon its capture in the December of this year (1810),
and Captains Willoughby, Pym, Curtis, and Lambert
were tried by court-martial and honourably acquitted,
and of Captain Willoughby's conduct specially the
Court expressed its opinion that he " carried the
Nereide into battle in a most judicious, officer-like,
and gallant manner, and the Court cannot do otherwise than express its high admiration of the noble

conduct of the captain, officers, and ship's company
during the whole of the unequal contest." Captain
Willoughby lived to be knighted by her present
Majesty in the year she ascended the throne, twenty-
seven years after these events.

But we have not come to the end of the British
losses. Commodore Rowley, in the *Boadicea*, 38,
picked up the *Magicienne's* barge, from which he
learned of the unfortunate issue of the attack on
Grand Port, and, accompanied by the *Otter*, 16, Commander Tomkinson, and gun-brig *Staunch*, Lieutenant
Street, chased the *Astrée*, 40, and *Iphigenia*, now a
French cruiser, and soon after sighted the *Africaine*,
38, Captain Corbett, just arrived from England. The
Africaine outsailed her consorts, and fearful that the
French frigates would return to Port Louis, Captain
Corbett engaged them alone. The action began at
2.20 A.M., but the second broadside of the *Astrée*
mortally wounded Captain Corbett, when Lieutenant
Tullidge continued the unequal conflict with one ship
at pistol-shot on his port beam and another on his
starboard bow, raking him with rounds of grape.
Lieutenants Tullidge and Forder were both severely
wounded and taken below, and the master was killed
by a round shot, and soon the *Africaine* was reduced
to a wreck, while no help could come from the
Boadicea, which lay becalmed five or six miles off.
At five o'clock she struck her colours, when of 295

men on board, including 25 soldiers, 49 were killed
and 114 wounded, including almost every officer. A
breeze soon after sprung up, and the *Boadicea*, being
joined by the *Otter* and *Staunch*, bore up for the
enemy, who had abandoned the *Africaine*, which
was recaptured as she lay with bowsprit and masts
over the side. The *Ceylon*, 32 (late Indiaman *Bombay*), Captain Charles Gordon, at this time encountered
the 40-gun frigate *Venus* and the *Victor*, 16 (which
as the *Jena* had been taken in 1808 by the *Modiste*,
and retaken by the *Bellone* in the following year),
though the enemy was so superior to the British
frigate that resistance was hopeless.   Nevertheless,
Captain Gordon fought his ship all that night, but at
4.30 hauled down his colours with a loss of 10 killed
and 31 wounded.   Soon the *Boadicea* appeared upon
the scene, and after ten minutes' cannonade compelled
the *Venus* to strike, while the *Otter* and *Staunch* took
possession of the *Ceylon*.   These events occurred in
September, 1810, and, as I have said, in December
Mauritius surrendered to a combined military and
naval expedition, when in Port Louis were found three
captured Indiamen, 24 French merchantmen, and the
40-gun frigates *Bellone* (renamed *Junon*), *Astrée* (now
called *Pomone*), *Iphigenia*, and *Nereide*, which was
broken up, but to commemorate her grand defence
Admiral Bertie gave the *Ceylon* her name.

There was a good deal of desultory fighting during

the year 1811, and on one occasion the Emperor
Napoleon having embarked on board a " prame," or
armed gunboat, witnessed the capture of one of them
by the *Naiad*, 38, Captain Carteret, while much
fighting took place with the Danes, and the defence
of Anholt, in the Cattegat, which had been captured
in May, 1809, like that of the Diamond Rock in the
West Indies, was very meritorious.

The enemy here attacked with 12 gunboats and
1,000 men, but though the defending force was under
400 marines, the Danes were driven off. This year
was also memorable for the loss of the line-of-battle
ships *St. George* and *Defence* off the coast of Jutland,
and of the *Hero* near the Texel, when nearly 2,000
officers and seamen perished. On the other hand, it
is noteworthy for the brilliant victory achieved at Lissa
by Captain Hoste's three 38-gun frigates, *Amphion*,
Cerberus, and *Active*, with the *Volage*, 22, over Commodore Dubourdieu with the 40-gun frigates *Favourite*,
Danae and *Flore* and three Venetian frigates, *Corona*,
Bellone, and *Carolina*. The action began at 9 A.M.,
and two hours later the *Flore* struck to Captain
Hoste's ship, the *Amphion*, which then compelled
the *Bellone* to follow suit. Captain Gordon, of the
Active, after a chase closed on the *Corona*, which
surrendered, but the other ships escaped under the
protection of the batteries of Lessina. In this splendid
action against superior force Captain Hoste, who

commenced the action with the signal "Remember
Nelson," lost 15 killed and 47 wounded in his own
ship (himself among the latter), the *Cerberus* had 13
killed and 41 wounded, and Captain Hornby's ship,
the little *Volage*, which had gallantly engaged the
Danae, sustained a loss in the unequal action of 46,
including 13 killed.   The *Flore* after surrendering
escaped, the *Favourite* blew up, and the *Corona*
caught fire, but the allied loss was very heavy, the
Corona losing about 200, the *Favourite* the same,
and the *Bellone* having 70 killed alone.

On the other side of the account the 18-gun brig
Alacrity, after a protracted resistance, was surrendered
by the boatswain, all the other officers being *hors de
combat*, to the French brig *Abeille*, of equal force, one
of the few instances of such an occurrence.   The
commander went below when slightly wounded, but
Lieutenant Rees, who succeeded him, displayed great
heroism, and though desperately wounded remained
on deck animating his men until a second shot
stretched him lifeless on the deck.   But the year
closed with another success near the scene of his
former exploit, achieved by Captain Gordon, of the
Active, assisted by Captain Henry Maxwell, of the
Alceste, 38, an officer of the same enterprising
character.   After a six hours' chase the former
brought the *Pomone* to action, and the *Alceste*, the
Pauline, both 40-gun frigates, but having by a lucky

hit shot away the *Alceste's* main-topmast, her opponent made sail and escaped, though the *Pomone* surrendered to superior force, as Captain Maxwell ranged up at close quarters to the assistance of his consort. The gallant Gordon had his leg carried off by a cannon shot, and his first lieutenant, Dashwood, lost an arm, when the *Active* was brought out of action by Lieutenant Haye, who was also wounded, but it was to the *Active's* fire that the surrender of the *Pomone*, which had her masts shot away, was chiefly due. Both these officers as well as Lieutenant Wilson of the *Alceste* were promoted. On the same occasion the *Personne*, store ship of 26 guns, struck to the *Unité*, 36, after what Captain Chamberlayne describes as " a persevering resistance for nearly four hours."

The year 1812 was memorable for the outbreak of the war with the United States of America. It is perhaps forgotten that though now the French found a very efficient naval ally in the United States, in 1798 they had been embroiled in actual hostilities with that power at sea, for though the difficulties that arose between these nations were adjusted before war was declared, yet the American Government ordered their ships to attack those of the enemy, and on the 9th February, 1799, an engagement took place between the Yankee cruiser *Constellation*, carrying 50 guns and 440 men, and the 40-gun frigate *Insurgente*. After a spirited resistance of 75 minutes the

Frenchman, which had lost 29 killed and 44 wounded out of 340 on board, struck her flag, and great were the jubilations of the Americans over this victory, in which their well-wishers in England joined, and the merchants of London presented Commodore Truxton with a handsome piece of plate for having captured a frigate stated to be of " superior force." The *Constellation* on the 1st February in the following year engaged the *Vengeance*, 40, Captain Pichot, and a running fight ensued from eight in the evening until one next morning, when the *Constellation*, owing to the damaged state of her rigging and spars, fell astern and the *Vengeance* escaped. Yet a third action took place between American and French ships-of-war, when after a spirited resistance the *Berceau*, of 22 guns, surrendered to the 32-gun frigate *Boston*, Captain Little, but not until her commander was killed and she was reduced to a helpless condition, the *Boston* also being much damaged.

War was declared between England and the United States in June, 1812, but in May of the preceding year Commodore Rogers, of the *President*, 56, engaged the British 20-gun sloop-of-war *Little Belt*, and firing did not cease till Captain Bingham had lost 32 men killed and wounded in protecting the honour of his flag, for the unprovoked attack on which an apology was tendered. The first shot fired in the war was between the British 38-gun frigate *Belvidera* and the

President, commanded by Commodore Rogers, when, after a running fight of two hours, Captain Byron was glad to make his escape, as the *Congress*, of 36 guns, arrived to the assistance of the so-called Yankee frigate, for the *President*, like the *Constitution* and *United States*, though rated as a 44, carried 56 guns, and was in reality a 74-gun ship cut down, hence called *rasées*, which carried 24-pounders on the main deck, and elsewhere 18-pounders and carronades throwing a 42-pound shot, with a complement of 476 officers and men. The superiority in crew and weight of metal, and let us add, in some instances, also in gunnery, received a disastrous illustration in the action between the *Constitution*, Captain Hall, and the 48-gun frigate *Guerrière*, commanded by Captain Dacres, an old French prize. The *Guerrière* fired the first shot at 4.30 P.M. on the 19th August, 1812, and within an hour and a half was dismasted and reduced to the condition of a wreck. The *Constitution*, taking up a position on her bow, first raked her with terrible effect, and then fouling her attempted to board, but was repulsed. Captain Dacres, though wounded, refused to quit the deck, and it was not until he recognised that further resistance only entailed a useless expenditure of life, as his ship, rolling in the trough of the sea, presented an easy mark to the enemy, but could make no effective return, that he hauled down his flag from the stump of the mizen-mast. Out of 263 officers and men with which she went into action 15 were killed and 63 wounded, and that the defence had been adequate was proved by the *Guerrière* being so riddled with shot that she could no longer float and was burnt by her captors.

We will only briefly chronicle the capture of the *Alert*, 16, by the United States frigate *Essex*, carrying 46 guns, and add that the latter had in turn to strike eighteen months later, to the combined attack of the *Phœbe*, Captain Hillyar, carrying 42 guns, and 24-gun ship *Cherub*. The Yankee had been blockaded in Valparaiso, but escaping to sea was brought to action, and struck after a very gallant defence (of which an account is given in the life of the celebrated American Admiral Farragut), with the loss of 24 slain and 45 wounded. Now came a succession of defeats, the first to surrender being the 18-gun brig *Frolic*, Commander Whinyates, which, while in a crippled state aloft from the effects of a recent gale, was engaged by the corvette *Wasp*, of 18 guns and 138 men, which had just put to sea from the Delaware, her opponent having been five years in commission. The *Frolic* surrendered after 45 minutes' resistance, having sustained a loss, out of 109 all told, of 15 killed and 47 wounded, including her captain, both lieutenants (one mortally), and her master, who also died of his wound. A few hours afterwards both the prize and her victor fell into the hands of the *Poictiers*, 74, which hove in sight.

A week later the 38-gun frigate *Macedonian*, Captain Carden, encountered the *United States*, and a sanguinary action ensued between these ill-matched combatants, but within a couple of hours the British frigate lost her mizen-mast and fore and main-top-masts, and being unmanageable, Captain Carden resolved to adopt the desperate expedient of boarding a ship of greatly superior force. But he failed to get alongside, and as his ship could no longer fight her main-deck guns, the muzzles of which were rolling under water, he hauled down the Union Jack, whose honour had been well defended, for out of 289 men and boys 36 had been killed and 68 wounded. It was some satisfaction to Captain Carden to find, on being removed to the enemy, that a large number of her crew were British seamen, among them being some who had manned the *Victory's* barge. As disastrous was the action between the 38-gun frigate *Java* (late French prize *Renommée*), under Captain Lambert, and the *Constitution*, now commanded by Captain Bainbridge. The *Java* was on her way to Bombay with General Hyslop and his staff and a quantity of military stores, when, on the 30th December, she was brought to close action by the Yankee. The Java had the misfortune to lose her bowsprit, so that she manœuvred with difficulty, and this was followed by the loss of her foremast, when, as she lay helplessly, the *Constitution* poured in her broadsides where she liked, and nothing remained to Lieutenant Chads, who had succeeded Captain Lambert on that officer being mortally wounded, but to surrender the British frigate. Out of a crew of 300 men, besides 86 supernumeraries, she had lost 22 killed, including six officers, and 102 wounded ; but that the requirements of honour had been fulfilled was proved by the fact of the *Java* being so damaged that she had to be set on fire. Lieutenant Chads was highly eulogised for his gallant conduct, and lived to perform excellent service in the Burmese war twelve years later.

Further disasters were sustained by the British navy. The *Peacock*, 18, Commander Peake, who was slain, was captured by the 20-gun corvette *Hornet*, Captain Lawrence, and so shot-riddled was the former that she sank almost immediately after. Then the schooner *Dominica* was taken by the privateer *Decatur*, and the 14-gun brig *Boxer*, Commander Blyth, became the prize of the *Enterprise*, 16, with double her crew, when both the captains fell in the desperate encounter. In the case of the *Dominica*, which was carried by boarding, her crew and that of the *Decatur*, numbering 66 and 120 respectively, the former lost no less than 18 killed, among whom were her gallant commander, Lieutenant Barretté (who, though wounded in two places, refused to surrender, and died fighting), and four other officers, while 47 were wounded, including every other officer except the surgeon and a midshipman. The American 18-gun corvette *Peacock* followed up this defeat by capturing the *Epervier*, which, as usual, was of greater tonnage and carried a stronger crew. Even more unequal and sanguinary was the action between the *Wasp*, 18, and the 18-gun brig *Reindeer*, whose gallant commander, Manners by name, the idol of his crew, did all a brave man could do to retrieve the fortunes of the fight. But superior gunnery again told with fatal effect, and the *Reindeer*, falling foul of the *Wasp*, Captain Manners, who had been twice wounded, in desperation called on his men to board with him, when two musket-balls from the *Wasp's* top passed through his head and he fell dead on the deck. The Americans now boarded and captured the brig, which had to be burnt, as she was a wreck aloft and cut to pieces in her hull. Her loss, out of 118, was 25 killed and 45 wounded, and the *Wasp*, whose complement was 173, had 11 in the former category and 15 in the latter. The *Wasp* a few months later took the *Avon*, of the same force as the *Reindeer*, which lost her first lieutenant and nine men killed and 32 wounded, including Captain Arbuthnot, but the British brig went down soon after the action, and the *Wasp* also foundered a few weeks later in a hurricane, when every one of her gallant crew perished.

The list of losses is continued with the capture of the *Cyane*, 22, and *Levant*, 20, by the *Constitution*, after a protracted resistance ; of the schooner *St. Lawrence* by the privateer *Chasseur*, when half of the British crew were *hors de combat*, and of the *Penguin*, 18-gun brig, by the *Peacock*, corvette, her superior by four guns and 60 men. Commander Dickinson, of the *Penguin*, did all a brave officer could effect, and in despair sought to board the enemy, but was mortally wounded, and at length the brig struck her colours, with the loss of 10 killed and 28 wounded. This dreary catalogue of defeat was relieved by three successes. The 18-gun brig *Pelican*, Commander Maples, captured the *Argus*, 20, and the 38-gun frigate *Endymion* made a prize of the *President*, whose captain, Decatur, had commanded the *United States* in her victory over the *Macedonian*. The *Endymion*, Captain Hope, had been repulsed in an attempt made by her boats to cut out an American 18-gun privateer, when no less than 28 men were killed, including Lieutenant Hawkins and a midshipman, and 37 were wounded ; but her crew had their revenge when, three months later, on the 15th January, 1815, they overhauled the *President*, which attempted to escape from the clutches of

a British squadron blockading New York, but surrendered after a smart action, though it should be
added in justice she actually struck to the *Pomone*
and *Tenedos*, which came up at the close of the action.
Still, her casualties were entirely attributable to the
accurate fire of the *Endymion*, which had 11 killed and
14 wounded, the *President*, out of a crew exceeding
hers by 156, losing three lieutenants and 32 killed
and 70 wounded, among whom was Commodore
Decatur.

But Captain Broke, of the 38-gun frigate *Shannon*,
was the hero of this Anglo-American war—on our
side, at least; and his victory over the *Chesapeake*
was one of the most remarkable and brilliant feats
recorded in war, and proved that it only needed
discipline and good training to ensure for British
crews a victory over Americans as over all other
maritime nations. The action took place off Boston,
on the 1st June, 1813, a glorious anniversary for
the British navy, and was the result of a challenge
from Captain Broke addressed to Captain Lawrence,
lately the gallant commander of the *Hornet*. The
superiority in size, weight of metal, and crew was all
on the side of the Yankee, though not to any great
extent, and it is a remarkable fact that, eight months
before the action, the following lines appeared in the
Naval Chronicle, which showed the writer was a
prophet as well as a bard :—

" And as the war they did provoke,
    We'll pay them with our cannon ;
  The first to do it will be Broke,
    In the gallant frigate *Shannon*."

The *Chesapeake* sailed out of Boston at noon to meet her antagonist, which lay in the offing, and it was exactly 5.50 when the first shot was fired by the discharge of the *Shannon's* 14th, or aftermost, main-deck gun, which took effect on the second main-deck port from forward of the Yankee frigate, at which it was aimed. Immediately a rapid cannonade ensued, every shot from the skilful gunners of the *Shannon* striking its mark. As the enemy, who was losing heavily, appeared to be about to board, Captain Broke, desirous of equalising the numbers before their intention was carried into effect, though he had marked out for himself the same part, starboarded his helm to keep the ship off the wind, when her jib-stay was shot away, in consequence of which the *Chesapeake* fell on board the *Shannon*, her quarter port hooking the fluke of the latter's starboard anchor. This was exactly at 6 P.M., and Captain Broke, observing the Americans leaving the quarter-deck guns, ran forward, and giving orders to lash the ships together and cease firing, called away the boarders under the first lieutenant, Watt, and at two minutes past the hour of six, the gallant Broke stepped from the gangway-rail just abaft the fore-rigging on to the muzzle of the *Chesapeake's* after-

"THE GALLANT BROKE STEPPED FROM THE GANGWAY RAIL."

most carronade, and vaulted over the bulwark on to
her quarter-deck with 20 men by his side. Not an
enemy was there to oppose him, but about 30 were
assembled on the gangways, who were driven forward
over the bows into the sea or laid down their arms
on the forecastle. Lieutenant Watt quickly followed
his captain, but was shot by a musket-ball from the
mizen-top, and Broke was joined by Lieutenant Falk-
iner, the third lieutenant (Lieutenant Provo Wallis
remaining on board the *Shannon*), when all rushed
forward, and while one party kept below the
men ascending the main hatchway, another party
replied to the fire from the main and mizen-tops.
In the meantime the *Shannon's* veteran boatswain,
Stevens (who had fought in Rodney's action on the
12th April, 1782), while in the act of lashing his
ship to the enemy, was mortally wounded by musketry, his left arm being also hacked off by repeated
cutlass blows, and the midshipman commanding on
the forecastle, Mr. Samwell, also fell. But at the
same time the *Chesapeake's* main-top was stormed
by Midshipman Smith, with five men, who ran along
the fore-yard and so on to the enemy's mainyard,
while the fire of their mizen-top was silenced. All
resistance was now over, when the men who had
surrendered to Captain Broke treacherously attacked
him, but they were all put to the sword. In his
hand-to-hand encounter Broke was opposed to three

men, one of whom he wounded, but was himself cut down, though his life was saved by Windham, the captain of the gun who had fired the first shot in the action, just as he was about to be despatched.

Thus the *Chesapeake* was the prize of the *Shannon* in exactly fifteen minutes after the commencement of the action and four from the time of boarding ; but though brief, the struggle had been desperate and sanguinary, for 24 of her gallant crew, including Lieutenant Watt and two other officers, had fallen, and 59 were wounded. The superior precision of the British fire was displayed in the comparative damage inflicted, for whereas the *Shannon* had suffered little, the hull of the *Chesapeake* was severely battered, and her rigging and masts much cut up. Of 386 men (56 more than the crew of her opponent), she lost a lieutenant, the master, four other officers, and 41 seamen and marines killed and 105 wounded, among whom were her captain and first lieutenant (both mortally), the other two lieutenants and six officers. Altogether the victory was as glorious and creditable to Captain Broke and his crew as any recorded in war, and equally gallant was the conduct of Captain Lawrence, who died two days after the action, but his men, although a picked crew, were not equal either in skill or daring to their adversaries.

During the remainder of the war with France the frigate actions were neither very numerous or im-

portant, but some were very hard-fought, and others
were drawn. Such was the engagement off Madagascar,
between the 36-gun frigates *Astrea*, *Phœbe*, and
Galatea, Captains Schomberg, Hillyar, and Losack,
and the 18-gun brig *Racehorse*, Commander de Rippe,
and the 40-gun frigates *Renommée*, *Clorinde*, and
Neréide, each carrying 200 soldiers in addition to their
crews. The action commenced at 4 o'clock, but
owing to the wind having fallen to a calm, the *Clorinde* and *Renommée*, finding themselves in a favourable position across the quarter and stern of the
Phœbe and *Galatea*, opened a most destructive fire,
to which they could give scarcely any reply. The
Phœbe had also the *Neréide* on her starboard bow,
whose fire she silenced, but the *Galatea*, which had
been terribly battered, could scarcely return any
effective fire, though at length, with the aid of her
boats, she was enabled to bring her broadside to bear,
when a breeze having sprung up the two French
frigates made sail. The *Galatea*, however, was too
crippled to pursue, but closed on the *Astrea*, which,
with the *Phœbe*, bore up towards the enemy. Shortly
before 10 P.M., Captain Hillyar closely engaged the
Renommée, which struck to the *Phœbe*, after receiving a few raking shots from the *Astrea*. The *Clorinde*
left her consort to her fate and returned to France,
reaching Brest in safety ; but her commander was
tried by court-martial for deserting Commodore

Roquebert, and was sentenced to dismissal and three
years' imprisonment. The *Neréide*, the third frigate,
made sail for Tamatave, whither the *Astrea*, *Phœbe*,
and *Racehorse* (which had taken no effective part in
the action) proceeded, and to a summons the French
commander surrendered his ship and the fort. The
Galatea, which suffered most, had 55 shot-holes in
her hull, and lost 16 killed and 48 wounded, and the
Phœbe and *Astrea* between them nine and 40 respectively, while the *Renommée* had 145 casualties, including the Commodore killed, and the *Neréide* 130.

A brilliant victory was gained off Venice by the
Victorious, 74, Captain Talbot, over the *Rivoli* of
the same force. The two ships were running side
by side under a press of sail while a furious cannonade raged, but at the end of four hours, when the
mizen-mast of the French 74 had been shot away,
she struck her colours, the 18-gun brig *Weasel*
having first fired two broadsides into her. In this
creditable affair the *Victorious* had an officer and 25
men killed and 93 wounded, including Captain
Talbot (who was knighted) and five officers, while the
Rivoli was terribly shattered, and lost no less than
400 *hors de combat*. As sanguinary, having regard
to the numbers engaged, was the action between the
Southampton, 38, and the *Améthyste*—lately a French
frigate, now in the Haytian service—with 44 guns
and 700 men of various nationalities. Sir James

Yeo's summons to surrender having been refused, he opened fire, and in seventy-five minutes shot away the masts and bowsprit of his opponent, whose loss was no less than 105 killed and 120 wounded, including her gallant captain, Gaspard by name.

During the years 1812-3 numerous boat attacks were made, especially in the Adriatic, in Chesapeake and Delaware Bays, at New Orleans, and on the Canadian lakes, when desperate fighting took place; but want of space prevents me from even giving the barest details of them, though the dashing gallantry of the British officers and seamen engaged was as conspicuous as when Nelson and Cochrane were among the shining lights of the service, and in European waters at least their valour was rewarded with success. The year 1813 closed with a desperate but indecisive engagement between the *Amelia* and *Arethuse*, frigates of nearly equal force, though the former had a slight superiority in weight of metal and the Frenchman in men. The ships met off the coast of Africa, and, as so often happened, the action took place at night, there being bright moonlight, with a smooth sea and light wind. The *Arethuse* fired the first shot at 7.45, and soon Captain Irby fell on board his enemy, whose marksmen opened a heavy fire of musketry from her tops; but the ships got clear, though a second time they fouled and lay alongside each other, engaging furiously, with the muzzles of the guns almost touching. The crews actually snatched the sponges out of each other's hands and cut at one another with their cutlasses, while the *Arethuse's* marines by their fire swept the quarterdeck of the British frigate clear of officers and men, among those who fell being the two senior lieutenants, Bates and Pope, and a marine officer, while Captain Irby was severely wounded, and gave up the command to Lieutenant Wells, who was shortly afterwards killed, when the Master, Mr. de Mayne, assumed charge, but did not escape unscathed. The ships now parted, and the crews being too exhausted to renew the struggle, the action may be called a drawn one, both sides, as usual, claiming the victory. In this desperate duel the *Amelia* lost 51 killed, including seven officers, and 90 wounded, of whom 11 hailed from the quarter-deck. The captain of the French frigate, M. Bouvet, one of the best officers, it need scarcely be said, in the French service, acknowledged to a loss of 31 killed and 74 wounded, almost every officer, as in the case of the *Amelia*, being in the list of casualties.

There were a few notable frigate actions in 1814. The French 40-gun frigates *Iphigénie* and *Alcmène* were captured, the latter by the *Venerable*, when Captain Villeneuve, designedly or not is unknown, fell athwart-hawse the 74, on which Captain Worth boarded and compelled him to surrender his ship,

which lost 32 killed and 50 wounded, including the
gallant commander.   Meanwhile the *Cyene*, 22,
Captain Forrest, engaged her consort, and, sticking
close to her between the 16th and 20th January,
at length had his valour and perseverance rewarded
by the arrival of the *Venerable*, when the enemy
surrendered.   The two captured frigates were re-
named the *Gloire* and *Immortalité*.   The 36-gun
frigates *Creole*, Captain Mackenzie, and *Astrea*,
Captain Eveleigh, brought to action the 40-gun
frigates *Etoile* and *Sultane*, which had before chased
the *Severn*, but the *Creole*, having her masts and
rigging cut up, abandoned the action.   The *Astrea*,
however, closely engaged the *Etoile*, which raked
her severely fore and aft, but Captain Eveleigh,
backing round, came alongside, and a hot engagement ensued, the ships having their yards almost
locked.   The *Sultane*, passing to leeward, gave her
consort some assistance, but then made sail, and the
Etoile soon followed her, leaving the *Astrea* too
much damaged to pursue.   The British frigates lost
19 killed, including the gallant Eveleigh, and 63
wounded, and the enemy considerably more.   Two
months later the *Hebrus*, 36, Captain Palmer, after a
chase of seventeen hours' duration, brought the
Etoile to action, which, after a close and obstinate
engagement of over two hours, struck her colours,
but not before her hull was much shattered and she

had lost 40 killed and 73 wounded—sufficient evidence that Captain Phillibert had done his duty. In achieving this brilliant capture of a ship of equal force, the *Hebrus* sustained a loss of Midshipman Crawley and 12 men killed and 25 wounded. At the same time the *Sultane* struck to the *Hannibal*, 74, and earlier in the year the *Ceres* surrendered, after a running fight, to the *Tagus* and *Niger*, all the three captured frigates being added to the navy, the *Ceres* as the *Seine* and the *Sultane* as the *Topaze*. The *Ceres'* consort, *Clorinde*, now again at sea, was brought to action, after a long chase, by the *Eurotas*, 38, Captain Phillimore, who was dangerously wounded early in the conflict, the command devolving on Lieutenant Smith, who fought the enemy with obstinacy, the ships lying alongside each other. The *Eurotas* lost her fore and main-masts, and the *Clorinde* her main and mizen-masts, thus equalising the conditions of the conflict, but the enemy had no stomach for further fighting, and made sail. The crew of the British ship employed the night in refitting, and, this completed, gave chase, but they were robbed of the fruits, if not the honours, of victory, by the appearance of the *Dryad*, 36, to which the *Clorinde* struck her colours, her acknowledged loss having been 30 killed and 40 wounded, though the British estimate placed it higher, while the *Eurotas* had 21 killed, including three midshipmen, and 39 wounded. The prize was added to the navy as the *Aurora*, there being a *Clorinde* already in the service. This action, which took place in February, 1814, was the last between British and French frigates in what may be called the heroic period of our navy's history. This history —briefly as its stirring incidents have been necessarily described owing to the exigencies of space— has been written in vain unless the reader is animated, after its perusal, with an increased admiration for the heroism, seamanlike skill, and determination, at all hazards, to perform their duty, displayed by our seamen, in the execution of which so many thousands died, finding, like the myriads of their countrymen who perished at sea, a sailor's grave.

> " But though no stone may tell
>   Their name, their work, their glory,
> They rest in hearts that loved them well,
>   And grace Britannia's story."